TEACHING SHAKESPEARE

D1332387

Teaching Shakespeare

Essays on approaches to Shakespeare in schools and colleges

Collected and edited by

Richard Adams

Robert Royce

First published 1985
Copyright © Richard Adams and contributors 1985
Robert Royce Limited, 93 Bedwardine Road, London SE19 3AY

British Library Cataloguing in Publication Data
Teaching Shakespeare: essays on approaches to
  Shakespeare in schools and colleges.
  1. Shakespeare, William—Study and teaching
  I. Adams, Richard, *1938–*
  822.3'3   PR2987

ISBN 0 947728 14 7

Phototypeset by Input Typesetting Ltd, London
Printed and bound in Great Britain by
Biddles Ltd, Guildford and King's Lynn

Contents

Preface

This book offers ideas, information and practical advice on working with Shakespeare to teachers who feel in need of help in bringing the plays more vibrantly alive, whether in the classroom or the drama workshop. It does not present a single cure-all prescription for counter-acting all Shakespeare-teaching ills. The contributors – who for the most part are involved in widely different areas of education – have set out to describe individual approaches and methods that they have found helpful in their own work. Many, if not all, of these methods have the advantage of being easily adaptable and readers are encouraged to try out their own variations on suggested themes.

The range offered here is wide: Neil King's focus is on ways of introducing Shakespeare effectively to young teenagers, John Saunders's on finding a valid alternative to essay-writing as a means of responding to the plays. Peter Hollindale thinks about ways of easing the problems of studying Shakespeare at A level, while Peter Reynolds is concerned to encourage in those who read the printed texts a special awareness of what they imply about the stage action. Stage action lies at the centre of Braham Murray's argument, which sets out to draw parallels between teaching a play and directing it on the stage. John Wain's account of the nature of

Shakespeare's realism will be found of particular value by those who are constantly on the look out for new ways of conveying the freshness and relevance of the plays to young audiences.

Three further essays provide help in more immediately practical ways: Ken Warren defuses some of the worries encountered by pupils facing examinations at 16+ and 18+ by explaining what examiners are looking for in the questions they set on Shakespeare's plays; Susan Macklin reviews some of the excellent books on teaching and studying Shakespeare that have appeared during the last decade; and Linda Cookson assesses the merits of various currently available school and academic editions of the plays. Bob Fowler's postscript is a personal reflection on Shakespeare as travelling companion.

Notes on the contributors

RICHARD ADAMS has behind him twenty-one years of experience as a teacher both in school and university. His work on Shakespeare includes editions of *Richard II, Richard III* and *Antony and Cleopatra* as well as the influential *Into Shakespeare* (an introduction to Shakespeare through drama) on which he collaborated with Gerard Gould. Now a professional writer and lecturer, he divides his time between Oxford and San Francisco.

LINDA COOKSON teaches at Lord Williams's School, Thame. She has published a number of short stories and has been responsible for editions of *Doctor Faustus, Wuthering Heights* and *Nineteen Eighty-Four* (all for Longman) and for York Notes on *Nightmare Abbey* and *Crotchet Castle*. She is also author of *Writing*, published by Hutchinson.

BOB FOWLER is an HMI with national responsibility for drama and a member of the Arts Council Drama Advisory Panel. Before joining the Inspectorate he was Warden of Bretton Hall, then Head of English and Drama at Sittingbourne College of which he later became Deputy Principal. His published works include *Themes in Life and Literature, The Hobbit: introduced for schools, English – a literary foundation course* (with

A. J. B. Dick) and *English 11–16* (5 volumes, also with A. J. B. Dick).

PETER HOLLINDALE taught at King's School, Gloucester and Clifton College before taking up an appointment at the University of York, where he is Senior Lecturer in English and Education. He has been involved in in-service work on Shakespeare teaching at courses run by the DES and by local authorities. He is General Editor of the Macmillan Shakespeare, and has himself published editions of *As You Like It* and *Henry IV Part One*, as well as a critical study of *Henry IV Part Two*.

NEIL KING has taught in schools in Stockton-on-Tees, Watford, Bushey and Cambridge, and has been an examiner in English Literature for five different examination boards. At present he is Senior English Master at Hymers College, Hull, and is engaged on research into aspects of moral and dramatic tension in Elizabethan and Jacobean Revenge Tragedy. He has compiled a drama series for schools which covers all aspects of the theatre from the Greeks to the twentieth century, has edited *She Stoops to Conquer* for Longman, is the author of York Notes on *Everyman, The Duchess of Malfi, The Revenger's Tragedy, The Changeling* and *The Relapse*, and has written and co-authored plays which have been performed at Durham, Hull, Cambridge and the Edinburgh Festival.

SUSAN MACKLIN has been a Senior Lecturer in Drama at Homerton College, Cambridge, since the early nineteen–seventies. Her previous experience includes teaching English and Drama in secondary schools and lecturing in Drama at Goldsmith's College, London. She has edited *The Rivals* for Longman.

BRAHAM MURRAY is Resident Artistic Director at Manchester's Royal Exchange Theatre. He made his first impact on British Theatre while still a student at Oxford, as co-author and director of *Hang Down your Head and Die* – an anti-capital-punishment documentary musical which transferred to the West End in 1964 (winning the Variety Critics' Award) and then to Broadway. Since then he has been closely associated with the Century and 69 theatre companies, directing for the latter such successful productions as *Charley's Aunt* (with Tom Courtenay), *Mary Rose* (with Mia Farrow), *Endgame* and the Shakespeare musical *Catch My Soul* – all of which transferred to London. Also in the West End, he directed André Previn's version of Priestley's *The Good Companions* (with John Mills and Judi Dench) and the highly praised *Black Mikado*. In Manchester, Braham Murray has in recent years been responsible for *The Dybbuk, The Rivals, What the Butler Saw, The Winter's Tale, Measure for Measure* and *Waiting for Godot*. In 1983 he directed *Hamlet* (with Robert Lindsay) in a production which toured England in the company's new mobile theatre, finishing with a three–week run on the roof of the Barbican Centre.

PETER REYNOLDS trained as an actor at the Central School of Speech and Drama, and later read English at the University of Sussex. He has worked in the professional theatre in England and the United States of America. Currently he is Lecturer in Drama at the Roehampton Institute, and has just completed *Text into Performance*, a book dealing with the process whereby dramatic literature is translated into a theatrical event, which Penguin are publishing early in 1986.

JOHN SAUNDERS has taught English at Bulmershe College and Bishop Otter College, and is currently on the staff of the West Sussex Institute. His postgraduate research was on the subject of Shakespeare's text and he has published an edition of *Measure for Measure* (U.L.P.) He is an awarder in English Literature, both O and A level, for the Oxford and Cambridge Joint Examinations Board.

JOHN WAIN's close involvement with Shakespeare began in 1944, when he acted the part of Claudio in Nevill Coghill's production at Oxford of *Measure for*

Measure (the part of Angelo was played by Richard Burton). His passion for Shakespeare, both on the printed page and in the theatre, began then and has never diminished. In thirty years as a professional writer he has contributed now and again to Shakespearean criticism, sometimes by dramatic reviews in the *Observer*, sometimes by essays, in his book *The Living World of Shakespeare* (1964) and his volumes on *Macbeth* and *Othello* in Macmillan's 'Casebooks in Literature' series.

KEN WARREN has taught English in secondary schools and a college of education. He examined at O level for the Cambridge Board and the Southern Joint Board; he has been concerned with A level examining with the Associated Examining Board since 1965, for some time as Chief Examiner, and he currently moderates all three AEB A level English schemes. With the same board he was involved in the planning of the Theatre Studies syllabus. He is a member of the Secondary Examinations Council's 18+ English Committee which has, as one of its main concerns, the oversight and development of A level English examining.

He has always enjoyed teaching Shakespeare and has done his best to shatter the myth that examinations wreck the study of literature. He is firmly of the belief that the teacher and the examiner have complementary roles and that both contribute on equal terms to the effective study and appreciation of the plays.

Shakespeare in School – The state of play

RICHARD ADAMS

Of the barriers that stand between today's school pupils and a full understanding and enjoyment of Shakespeare, two in particular seem to me both significant and inter-related. They are an uncomprehending yet unquestioning awe of the playwright and a lack of familiarity with the medium in which he worked. It is, ironically, arguable that while most adults who see the plays in performance experience them in no other form, most children are introduced to them at school primarily as literary objects. We have a family story about an elderly relative who, having been informed that she was to be dragged along to a performance of *Julius Caesar* – a play about which she knew nothing and in which she had next to no interest – insisted on appearing in the stalls at Stratford hideously overdressed: 'a mark,' as she put it, 'of respect to Shakespeare, who is, after all, the world's greatest writer'. Pupils often approach enforced study of a Shakespeare play in a similar frame of mind; though they may actually be bored to distraction by reading *A Midsummer Night's Dream* round the class or puzzling out the meaning of

My hounds are bred out of the Spartan kind:
So flewed, so sounded; and their heads are hung
With ears that sweep away the morning dew;

1

Crook-kneed, and dewlapped like Thessalian
bulls;
Slow in pursuit, but matched in mouth like
bells,
Each under each[1]

with the aid of a forbidding array of glossary and notes,
they are conditioned to accept that such brushes with
greatness, like some potent but ill-tasting medicine, are
good for them.

Of course, awe of Shakespeare derives ultimately from
a long-standing recognition of his genius. As J.
Middleton Murry points out, he has been a classic of the
playhouse or of the library or of both for nearly four
centuries, the only periods when he suffered relative
neglect being those of the Commonwealth and the Restoration.[2] And throughout those four centuries there have
been those who have acknowledged his standing in tones
of religious fervour:

Call it worship, call it what you will, is it not a right
glorious thing and set of things, this that Shakespeare has brought us? For myself, I feel that there
is actually a kind of sacredness in the fact of such a
man being sent into this Earth. Is he not an eye to
us all; a blessed heaven-sent Bringer of Light?[3]

It was on account of his exasperation with the cult
of Shakespearean infallibility that George III made his
famous outburst in Fanny Burney's hearing:

'Was there ever,' cried he, 'such stuff as great part
of Shakespeare? Only one must not say so!'[4]

Samuel Johnson identified the problem with rather
greater finesse when he wrote in his *Preface to Shakespeare* (1765):

It must be at last confessed that, as we owe everything to him, he owes something to us; that, if much
of our praise is paid by perception and judgment,
much is likewise given by custom and veneration.[5]

We are all too ready, he points out, to acknowledge the

strengths and felicities in Shakespeare, but turn a blind eye to his 'deformities', pretending that they do not exist. We put up with things in him that in other writers we would be quick to 'loathe or despise'.

The unquestioning acceptance of Shakespeare's preeminence – and particularly his literary preeminence – was famously at its height during the nineteenth century. When, in 1880, Matthew Arnold was asked to contribute an essay on the study of poetry to T. H. Ward's selection from *The English Poets*, he made it the occasion for discussing the individual merits of writers from widely different periods and social backgrounds. His survey ranged from Chaucer to Burns; it did not, however, touch on the poetry of Shakespeare, Milton and their contemporaries, because

> we all of us profess to be agreed in the estimate of this poetry; we all of us recognise it as great poetry, our greatest, and Shakespeare and Milton as our poetical classics. The real estimate, here, has universal currency.[6]

And, as Lionel Trilling points out, when Arnold came to draw up his roll of 'our chief poetical names' (Shakespeare, Milton, Spenser, Dryden, Pope, Gray, Goldsmith, Cowper, Burns, Coleridge, Scott, Campbell, Moore, Byron, Shelley, Keats), he appears to have been reflecting the degree of establishment and reputation generally accorded these poets, rather than expressing a personal preference.[7] Here was the regiment of the eternal greats, with Shakespeare – predictably – at their head. And it is with the twentieth century's continued and apparently unquestioning adherence to this 'great tradition' in literary studies that a number of influential critics and educational sociologists have taken issue.

In the opening chapter of his introduction to literary theory, Terry Eagleton devotes some time to considering exactly what we mean by 'literature'. He makes the observation that value judgments play a large part in determining what is or is not worthy of the name. Literature is a highly subjective commodity and accords with the attitudes of individuals and groups living under particular social conditions at particular times:

> Anything can be literature, and anything which is regarded as unalterably and unquestionably literature – Shakespeare, for example – can cease to be literature.[8]

Eagleton elaborates this idea by envisaging a future time when 'given a deep enough transformation of our history' a society might be produced which is unable to get anything at all out of Shakespeare. 'His works might simply seem desperately alien, full of styles of thought and feeling which such a society found limited or irrelevant.' 'Value', in other words, is a transitive concept, and

> the so-called 'literary canon', the unquestioned 'great tradition' of the 'national literature', has to be recognised as a *construct*, fashioned by particular people for particular reasons at a certain time.[9]

He acknowledges that certain works of literature seem to retain their status across the ages; however, he puts this down not to any absolute value they possess, but to the pure chance that succeeding generations have prized them for different reasons and in different ways. Homer was revered during the Middle Ages and he continues to be revered today. But the mediaeval Homer was very different from the modern. So also with the seventeenth and twentieth century attitudes to Shakespeare:

> different historical periods have constructed a 'different' Homer and Shakespeare for their own purposes, and found in these texts elements to value or devalue, though not necessarily the same ones.[10]

Eagleton concludes his chapter with reference to I. A. Richards's study *Practical Criticism* (1929) and to the experiment described in it in which Richards gave his students a batch of poems for unseen appreciation. What interests Eagleton is not the variableness of the responses produced but just how tight was the consensus of unconscious valuations which underlay the differences of opinion. He points out that this was inevitably the case because the habits of perception and interpretation shared by Richards and his pupils derived from a common socio-historical background: 'they were all . . . young, white, upper- or upper middle-class, privately educated English people of the 1920s.' The value-judgments by which we determine what for us is or is not 'literature' are not simply a matter of private taste, he suggests, but have a close relation to social ideologies, 'the assumptions by which certain social groups exercise and maintain power over others.'[11]

It is these very assumptions that sociologists have seen at work in the formulation and urging of a literary curriculum as part of the teaching of English in schools since Victorian times. A glance at today's advanced level examination syllabuses can leave us in no doubt that the 'chief poetical names' identified by Arnold are still thought by many to be essential reading for pupils aged 16 to 19. As Margaret Mathieson has shown in her study of English and its teachers, *The Preachers of Culture*, Arnold and his contemporaries – men like Henry Sidgwick and G. C. Bradley – advocated the study of what was thought of as great literature because they believed firmly in its power to humanise. Sigdwick put it in this way:

> Let us demand . . . that all boys . . . be really taught literature; so that as far as possible, they may learn to enjoy intelligently poetry and eloquence; that their views and sympathies may be enlarged and expanded by apprehending noble, subtle and profound thoughts, refined and lofty feelings; that some comprehension of the varied development of human nature may even abide with them, the source and essence of a truly humanising culture.[12]

The 1921 report on *The Teaching of English in England* (popularly known as the Newbolt Report) saw literary studies playing their part in promoting social unity. Rich and poor would come together through their involvement in a common culture. English literature was to be the means of contact with great minds, 'a channel by which to draw upon their experience with profit and delight, and a bond of sympathy between the members of a human society.'[13] At the same time, writers such as George Sampson were insisting that if working-class children were not provided with the benefit of literary contact they would grow into men and women obsessed with materialism:

> I am prepared to maintain, and indeed, do maintain without reservation and perhapses, that it is the purpose of education, not to prepare children for their occupations, but to prepare children against their occupations.[14]

The writers of past ages were to be the bulwark against the depressing effects of work (especially of the mechanical, industrial sort), of life in the smoky cities and their faceless suburbs, of an existence in which peoples' thinking was being done for them by advertising, the cinema and the press. For F. R. Leavis and his disciples in the 1930s, the practical criticism of literature was a means of training the mind against 'the environment' in all its manifestations:

> In an ordinary school, all the time a literary education is striving to sharpen percipience and to provide standards, it is fighting a running engagement against the environment.[15]

In recent years, there has been a notable reaction against such doctrines, particularly among left-wing educationists. The 'great tradition' is seen in the light of what M.F.D. Young – discussing the work of the Italian Marxist, Antonio Gramsci – describes as the imposition of an upper-class cultural hegemony on the working classes, who are thus prevented from thinking for themselves.[16] Linguistic competence, it is argued, should be the educational priority; the inclusion of literature in all pupils' curricula 'with the inevitable exclusion of working-class culture, implicitly supports the present social structure with all its inequalities.'[17] The so-called New Left's proposals for change include an emphasis on pupil-centred classroom experiences, a shift from school and

adult values to those held by pupils, and the subordi-
nation of traditional disciplines – including the study of
literature – to pupils' everyday experiences.

The ideological gulf which separates the New Left from
more conventional educational thinking on the matter
of teaching literature is highlighted by the views articu-
lated in a recent publication of the Department of
Education and Science, which proposes that most pupils
'should have experienced some literature and drama of
high quality, not limited to the twentieth century,
including Shakespeare'[18] by the time they reach the end
of their years of compulsory schooling. We have, furthermore, already noted how advanced level examination
syllabuses for the most part support the *status quo*.

In an article entitled 'The Museum of Eng. Lit.'[19] David
Self makes a number of pertinent observations about
the texts prescribed for advanced level examinations. He
points, for instance, to the fact that the range of authors
– the range, indeed, of individual works – represented is
extremely narrow. Such flexibility as there is seems to
be confined to the 'modern' end of the syllabuses. All
GCE boards make the study of one or two Shakespeare
plays compulsory, though even here the prescriptive
spectrum is limited. From his study of the papers set
over a number of years, Self comes to the conclusion that
'there is such a thing as an A level play' and cites *King
Lear, Antony and Cleopatra* and *A Winter's Tale* as the
top three favourites, narrowly displacing *Hamlet* and
Othello. Whether or not this suggests a lack of imagination on the part of the prescribing committees, the
silence of schools and individual teachers on the subject
might lead one to believe that they are satisfied with the
arrangement:

> With a few notable exceptions . . . it seems that it
> can be claimed with justification that the A level
> English Literature syllabuses are conservative.
> Whether such claims, no matter how vociferous in
> some quarters, indicate a widespread desire for
> change is another matter.

Self goes on to suggest three possible reasons for this

state of affairs: firstly, that teachers are happier with 'classic' works because they are themselves more familiar with them and have the added security of a reasonable body of critical backup; secondly, because the introduction of pupils to English literature up to the 16+ stage is at best highly selective, at worst sketchy, it may be thought desirable to focus their attention at A level on a restricted number of high-calibre works which are characteristic of their authors at their best ('to know *Measure for Measure* and *Cymbeline* but not one of the great tragedies is to have an eccentric view of Shakespeare'); thirdly, because examiners feel themselves to be under pressure from schools to set books of proven literary merit, those that are indisputably worthy of study in depth. All of which suggests that teachers bear as much responsibility for perpetuating the 'great tradition' as do the examination boards and the universities which – for the most part – control them.

It is worth noting at this point that representatives of the New Left in education take issue as much with what they see as the 'authoritarian' methods of testing achievement currently employed in GCE examinations as they do with the entrenched position of traditional literature courses. In defining the dominant characteristics of what he calls 'high-status knowledge', M.F.D. Young touches on features which can be seen at a glance to apply equally to the testing of that knowledge: first comes literacy, the emphasis on writing things down rather than talking about them; next is individualism and the avoidance of group work or 'co-operativeness'; third is the abstract nature of the knowledge involved and – linked to this – the 'unrelatedness' of the process to daily life and common experience.[20] It scarcely needs adding that these three emphases – literacy, individualism and abstraction – are least helpful in the presentation and understanding of works of drama, whether by Shakespeare or by any other playwright.

In the prefatory essay which Peter Shaffer supplied recently for educational editions of three of his plays (*The Royal Hunt of the Sun*, *Equus* and *Amadeus*) he has this to say:

The pages [of these volumes] contain the material of live theatre . . . [This material] is intended to be brought to physical life in a space which has to be animated afresh each time of playing, by the vibrations of the actors and by those of the spectators. A play, like justice, is preeminently a thing *seen* to be done.[21]

Shaffer's view is one with which most playwrights would sympathise. Willy Russell, presenting his play *Educating Rita* to a German audience, insisted:

I write my plays to be played, not to be studied; if that sounds ungrateful let me add that I don't object to study of the plays but they are not primarily written for this; for a playwright the medium is the performance whilst the book is merely a record of the text.

There is, of course, no knowing with certainty what Shakespeare's line on the matter might have been. Stanley Wells has demonstrated, in his wide-ranging study of literature and drama in sixteenth- and seventeenth-century England,[22] that the early printing of plays arose from a variety of motives. It was seen, variously, as a means of encouraging wider performance, of counteracting the influence of pirated versions by making the true text readily available, of consoling the unlucky playwright for lack of success in getting his work played in public, and of commemorating prestigious one-off performances. In published plays of what Wells refers to as the Tudor period (that is, up to 1576), the prefaces and dedicatory epistles that so often indicated 'literary' pretensions on the part of an author were frequently lacking, while stage directions and information on characters – so helpful to the reading as opposed to the acting of a play – were kept to a basic and unelaborated minimum. At the same time, some title-pages suggest that the reading of plays was regarded as a perfectly possible activity and stress the didactic, moralistic aspects of the works in question, with a possible eye – as Wells points out – on a potential school market. Evidence of playwrights coming to consider their works as literary achievements is rather fuller in the period after 1576, and some even went out of their way to make their scripts more presentable for publication by cutting frivolous or bawdy material. Even so, plays were generally printed with little care and without the benefit of authorial supervision. Wells also attaches great importance to the absence of the dedicatory epistles so common in the printing of self-consciously literary works. He draws attention to the fact that not one of Shakespeare's plays printed in his lifetime includes a dedication, epistle or commendatory poem – with the exception of the 1609 edition of *Troilus and Cressida*, which has an epistle devised by the printer – while *Venus and Adonis* and *Lucrece* (which between them went through seventeen editions by 1617) both contain Shakespeare's own dedication to the Earl of Southampton.

A landmark in the early history of play-printing was reached with the appearance in 1616 of Ben Jonson's *Works* – the culmination of their author's campaign to obtain literary respectability for the popular drama. Where earlier playwrights had sanctioned the cutting of unsuitable material for the purpose of publication, Jonson actually added to what had appeared on the stage. His lists of *dramatis personae* included thumbnail sketches of the characters portrayed, and, in the case of *Sejanus*, he went so far as to provide notes on his classical sources and a summary of the plot. The *Works* proclaimed Jonson's sympathies with a boldly-placed motto on the title-page:

neque me ut miretur turba, laboro:
contentus paucis lectoribus[23]

– a gesture which earned him the derision of a number of his professional colleagues. Wells goes on to speculate on the part played by Jonson's *Works* in inspiring the publication of the Shakespeare First Folio in 1623. It was surely not pure coincidence that Jonson himself should have been invited to provide the dedicatory poem to be set opposite Martin Droeshout's engraving of

Shakespeare on the title-page, and there is a distinctly literary emphasis in the address 'to the great Variety of Readers' with which John Heming and Henry Condell prefaced their edition. These are works, we are told, not merely to be read but to be judged:

> You will stand for your priuiledges wee know: to read, and censure. Do so. . .[24]

It is not the business of the editors to praise what they have collected – *that* is to be left to the readers:

> And there we hope, to your diuers capacities, you will finde enough, both to draw, and hold you: for his wit can no more lie hid, then it could be lost. Reade him, therefore; and againe and againe: And if then you doe not like him, surely you are in some manifest danger, not to vnderstand him. And so we leave you to other of his Friends, whom if you need, can bee your guides: if you neede them not, you can leade your selues, and others. And such Readers we wish him.

We note here the encouragement to study, the recognition of a need on the part of some for help in understanding, the suggestion that these are works which we will want to read and reread for the many felicities they contain. It is worth adding that Heming and Condell believed that they were supplying a need not just for interested intellectuals, but also for the barely literate: their address is to the whole range of the reading public 'from the most able, to him that can but spell'.

There is nothing in their preface, however, to suggest that Shakespeare's erstwhile colleagues were out to encourage a radical shift from play-going to solitary reading. Their book is essentially a supplement to, rather than a replacement of, the theatrical experience. It does, however, answer the need for accurate texts of the plays, the public having been for too long 'abus'd with diuerse stolne, and surreptitious copies, maimed, and deformed by the frauds and stealthes of inurious impostors.' The sick bodies are now cured, their limbs restored to health

11

and strength – though, unlike Jonson's *Works*, without the ultimate benefit of their author's supervision.

A third and slightly curious emphasis in this opening 'address' comes in the editors' insistence on readers paying for the privilege of reading their book. The fact that people are prepared to buy a book, their printer has told them, is the best recommendation it can possibly receive:

> Then how odde soeuer your braines be, or your wisdomes, make your licence, and spare not. Iudge your six pen'orth, your shillings worth, your fiue shillings worth at a time, or higher, so you rise to the iust rates, and welcome. But, what euer you do, Buy.

Could it be that the King's Men were beginning to feel the pinch of literature and were attempting some mild financial diversification to offset it? We can only conjecture. We can, indeed, only conjecture about a number of aspects of the relationship between text and performance during the sixteenth and seventeenth centuries, but one thing seems fairly certain, and that is that it was a much closer, more natural relationship – the four centuries of essentially literary tradition having barely begun – than exists today.

It is a return to something approaching that original relationship in our experience of Shakespeare that a number of influential critics have recently been urging. John Russell Brown, for instance, maintains that 'until a reader has developed a sense of the plays in performance, a text cannot be read as it should be.'[25] A purely literary approach can place barriers in the way of our understanding which it will be difficult to eradicate later. But once a play, by coming to life before our eyes on the stage, has begun to act upon our imaginations, we can return to the text 'with new and sharpened curiosity'. Brown fully recognises the importance of the text itself, of our being able to sift through and reflect on the printed words, to pause where we will or move back and forth making new connections and realising new truths. These are things we cannot do as we watch a stage performance, whatever the degree of our involvement in it might be. He acknowledges that we are more than justified in close analysis of the text: Shakespeare was, after all, no haphazard worker, his 'well-turnèd and true-filèd lines' were the product of judgment, not luck. The danger of insufficient attention to textual study is that we may be dazzled into responding quickly to the vitality of the lines, but fail to discover their more profound secrets. However, that textual study must take place in the context of our understanding how a play works on the stage. Why this should be is impressively demonstrated in Glynne Wickham's notes on the staging of Marlowe's plays:

> Events are telescoped with frenzied haste. In conse-
> quence the reader of these plays gains the
> impression that they are poorly constructed, oscil-
> lating unevenly between rhetorical scenes of
> sustained poetic brilliance combined with perceptive
> character delineation on the one hand and sketchy
> linking devices on the other. Literary criticism
> knows no way round this difficulty. I venture to
> suggest that the opera critic would know better; for
> few indeed are the operatic librettos which follow
> any other pattern; and what, in the libretto, looks
> like a lazy linking device takes on an altogether
> different air in the theatre when filled out with its
> full orchestral accompaniment. So too, where
> Marlowe is concerned, I think we must make greater
> allowance than is usually admitted for the ritualistic
> quality of the theatre in which he worked.[26]

If we insist on approaching works intended to be brought to life in Shaffer's 'animated space' as if they are exclusively literary objects, if we peer darkly at image-clusters and verse-patterns but remain blind to the electricity which sparks between actors and audience at each and every playing, we are bound not only to miss an important part of what the practised stage-writer intended but also to distort his meanings. It is not simply a question of prefacing the study of Shakespeare in school with a visit to the theatre or cinema, or with a raid on the audio-visual resource centre; what is needed is for pupils to come to terms with the plays through first-hand experience of the performance process. This might be achieved in a number of ways – by introducing (or reintroducing) group drama work as an integral part of what goes on in Shakespeare lessons, employing techniques similar to those advocated over a decade ago by David Adland;[27] by taking a key scene from a set text and asking pupils to work at staging it, making their own decisions in the course of doing so on matters of production (including casting, costume, set design) and interpretation; or – ideally – by running the study of a complete play alongside a full-scale production (with – perhaps – occasional changes of cast in the interests of fairness). Such techniques, of course, require much more time, energy, experience and imagination on the part of the teacher than reading round, explaining obscure textual references or preparing potted character-sketches are ever likely to do. But, practised more widely than they are at present, they would ensure a marked reduction in the number of George IIIs emerging from our schools in the future. Jonathan Miller made the point in a recent interview that he would never consider letting a child start by *reading* Shakespeare: 'imagine,' he declared, 'what it would be like having to learn English, by reading it!' The parallel is both neat and apt.

NOTES

1 Shakespeare, *A Midsummer Night's Dream*, Act 4, Scene 1, lines 117–22.

2 J. Middleton Murry, *Shakespeare*, London, 1936, pp 413–27.

3 Thomas Carlyle, 'The Hero as Poet. Dante; Shakespeare,' 1840. Reprinted in *English Critical Essays (Nineteenth Century)*, selected and edited by Edmund D. Jones, London, 1916.

4 recorded in Fanny Burney's Diary, 19th December 1785.

5 Samuel Johnson, *Preface to Shakespeare*, 1765.

6 Matthew Arnold, 'The Study of Poetry', from *Essays in Criticism (Second Series)*, London, 1888.

7 Lionel Trilling, *Matthew Arnold*, London 1939, p 379 *n*.

8 Terry Eagleton, *Literary Theory – an Introduction*, Oxford, 1983, p 10.
9 Eagleton, *op. cit.*, p 11.
10 Eagleton, *op. cit.*, p 12.
11 Eagleton, *op. cit.*, pp 15–16.
12 quoted in Margaret Mathieson, *The Preachers of Culture*, London, 1975, pp 33–4.
13 *The Teaching of English in England*, London (H.M.S.O.), 1921, pp 15 f.
14 George Sampson, *English for the English*, Cambridge, 1925 (quoted from 1952 edition, p 11.)
15 Denys Thompson, 'What Shall we Teach?', *Scrutiny*, Vol 2, No 4 (March 1934), p. 384.
16 M. F. D. Young, 'Curricula as Socially Organized Knowledge', in *Knowledge and Control*, London, 1971, p 28.
17 Mathieson, *op . cit.*, p 140.
18 D. E. S. Curriculum Matters (1), *English from 5 to 16*, London (H.M.S.O.), 2nd October 1984, p. 11.
19 David Self, 'The Museum of Eng. Lit.', *Times Educational Supplement*, 25th June 1982, p 24.
20 M. F. D. Young, *op. cit.*, p 38.
21 Peter Shaffer, *The Royal Hunt of the Sun*, edited by Peter Cairns, Longman Study Texts, Harlow, 1983, p vi.
22 Stanley Wells, *Literature and Drama with special reference to Shakespeare and his Contemporaries*, London, 1970.
23 'I do not work to be gaped at by the crowd, but am happy with a few readers.'
24 Charlton Hinman (ed.), *The Norton Facsimile: The First Folio of Shakespeare*, London and New York, 1968.
25 John Russell Brown, *Discovering Shakespeare*, London, 1981, p 75.
26 These appear in Wickham's *Shakespeare's Dramatic Heritage*, 1969, quoted at length in Wells, *op. cit.*, p 91.
27 David Adland's *Group Approach to Shakespeare*, four volumes covering, respectively, *Romeo and Juliet, The Merchant of Venice, Twelfth Night* and *A Midsummer Night's Dream*, is unfortunately now out of print. *Into Shakespeare*, by Richard Adams and Gerard Gould, an introduction to Shakespeare through drama published by Ward Lock in 1977, contains suggested approaches to scenes from twelve plays and outlines ways of overcoming the difficulties they throw up through rehearsal and performance.

The Nature of Shakespeare's Realism

JOHN WAIN

– Truly, I would the gods had made thee poetical.
– I do not know what 'poetical' is. Is it honest in deed and
    word? Is it a true thing?

As You Like It

– And I with my long nails will dig thee pig-nuts.

The Tempest

I

'Realistic' art, in its generally accepted sense, means art
that builds on a platform of the representational, even
the photographic. In literature, it signifies a book or a
play in which the characters speak in the recognisable
idiom of their place, time and social class. The impact of
such work depends on its being able to foster a sense of
involvement; the reader, or spectator, feels that he or
she has blundered without warning into the midst of
a situation that might very well be part of quotidian
experience, in familiar settings and among people
wearing familiar clothes and using familiar everyday
objects. The drama is heightened by the fact that it starts
at ground level.

On the face of it, Shakespeare is very far from being
a realistic writer. His plays are habitually set in foreign
countries (Italy, for preference) which very few of his
audience had visited and which, for that matter, Shakespeare himself had not visited; or in remote historical
periods; or in non-existent places like the sea-coast of
Bohemia; or symbolic, imaginative places like Prospero's
island or 'Illyria' or 'a wood near Athens'. His characters
speak some or all of their parts in verse, often elaborately
crafted and of intricate metaphorical structure. He wrote

before modern conventions of realism came in and he seems conscious of no unfulfilled need in consequence.

Nevertheless, Shakespeare, among his multiplicity of other gifts, was certainly a realist; there is a strand of his work to which no other term applies so readily; and it seemed to me there might be a use in picking out this strand and attending to it separately. Especially since the main thrust of this book is towards the classroom; it is designed to give ammunition to teachers who have the job of trying to interest present-day children in Shakespeare's work. These children watch television, and television has thrown its colossal weight behind a drama in which ordinary people can recognise their ordinary lives, in a way that neither of the previous forms of mass drama, cinema and radio, felt called upon to do. The quickest way to realise this is to look at the change it has brought about in the acting profession. Thirty years ago, actors and actresses had to have profiles; they had to be noticeably better-looking than you and me, unless they were 'character actors', in which case they had to be noticeably uglier, or at any rate of a more gnarled and individual appearance, than you and me. Nowadays, the stars of television – which *ipso facto* means the stars of theatre too, because they are the ones who get the jobs – are stars precisely because they look, talk, and hold themselves like everyone else. They represent the norm of the population, and (since professional players can do anything) they do so successfully even when they themselves are, as individual men and women, very far from the norm of the population. This is their skill, their 'mystery'.

Given that they have been dieted with drama of this kind since the dawn of their consciousness, how can modern children begin to get on to terms with Shakespeare? There must be some straightforward way of approach, and my own would be to begin by noting that Shakespeare, as a practical man of the theatre, an actor, a shareholder in the company, keenly interested in success and not at all in failure, was 'realistic' in the popular sense of the word, which means that he faced facts. And one of the facts that he faced was that, other things being equal, his audience would be tempted into the theatre far more easily if they were told that the story of the play was a story of Italy.

This should not surprise us. It is a characteristic of the popular audience to have a dream-environment and to demand that the stories it is offered should take place there. In the 1930s, when I was growing up in Stoke-on-Trent, the local population were very faithful to the cinema. Everyone went to 'the pictures' all the time. They took their dreams, their aspirations, their sexual preferences, their patterns of behaviour, from 'the pictures', and between visits they read a host of magazines which were satellites of the cinema industry. It never occurred to them that their world, in its imaginative dimension, could have any other centre. I remember a plaintive letter from a girl to the local newspaper, which began, 'I am absolutely fed up with the pictures, where I go five times a week.'

There would have been only one way, in the thirties, to keep the population out of the cinema, though of course no one was fool enough to try it, except in fringe cinema which, economically, didn't count. That way would have been to offer them a film that was not about America. To them, American life was the natural subject-matter of the cinema, almost to the extent that 'a film' meant 'a filmed story about America'. If it was a cops-and-robbers film, it was set in Chicago or New York. If it was a great-outdoors film, it was set in the Wild West. If it was a sophisticated film about the intrigues of rich, beautiful and witty people, it was set in California, and usually in Hollywood itself. My fellow-citizens of Stoke-on-Trent went to the cinema ('five times a week') to see films about America. If you had offered them a film set in Glasgow or London or Liverpool, they would have turned back at the door. A non-American film would have seemed to them a non-film, a contradiction in terms.

By keeping that simple fact in mind we are in a position to understand why Shakespeare made such a habit of setting his plays in Italy. During his working life, the audience, sophisticated and simple alike, thought of Italy as the audiences of my boyhood thought of America. It was the Place Where Things Happened.

By setting the majority of his plays in a dream-Italy, then, and giving the characters Italian names, Shakespeare was showing 'realism' in the popular sense of the word: he was facing facts, bowing to the inevitable. But he showed himself a master of other kinds of realism than the merely acquiescent. Those goals of authenticity, piercing honesty, and recognisable truth to the human condition, which are the ultimate objectives of realistic art, Shakespeare achieved in his own way.

The systematic pursuit of 'realism' in literature, whatever precise or shifting meaning we attach to that word, is a phenomenon of the modern world; not the world of space travel and information technology, but that of the railway train, the factory and the big city. As a critical term applied to both literature and painting, it dates from the 1850s; the painter Courbet put up a sign outside his one-man show in 1855 that read 'Du Réalisme', and in the following years Edmond Duranty tried, without much success, to launch a magazine of the arts called *Réalisme*. The magazine may not have lived but the movement did; Flaubert, whose *Madame Bovary* began to appear serially in 1856, is closer to the fully evolved norm of realism than Stendhal, just as Tolstoy, whose *Sevastopol* also began to come out in that same year, is closer to it than Gogol or Pushkin. Later in the century the term became politicised, and in our day 'Socialist Realism' is the official artistic doctrine of one half of the world, with real ('realistic'?) punishments awaiting those artists who do not conform to it.

What I personally mean by calling someone a realist I can perhaps explain. All the great story-tellers have known the value of the small prosaic fact that anchors a soaring imaginative vision to the everyday earth. Odysseus, on his return from his wanderings, is greeted by his old dog who has slept by the gate, awaiting his master in some recess of his mind, all those years. The most high-flown mediaeval romances have a way of suddenly coming down to concrete details about florins and loaves of bread. What marks off the fully realistic

writer, what was new about Realism as an official movement when it was first launched, was that it declared
these observations of quotidian reality to be the true, the
central, subject-matter of art.

The reasons for this *volte-face* lie in social history, and
fairly near the surface at that.

People who live very rooted lives, staying in one place,
doing work that is repetitive or at any rate cyclical, and
seeing one circle of acquaintances every day, tend to find
life humdrum. What they crave, when they are able to
get away from their work, is something that takes their
imagination out on a voyage. They want tales of the far
away, the marvellous, the unheard-of. People exactly
similar to themselves are not worth hearing stories about
except in those moments when their lives become
scandalous or hilarious. Hence the mediaeval alter-
nation between the lofty romance and the *fabliau*. There
was nothing between knights, giants and enchanters on
the one hand, and the custard pie and the adulterous
bed on the other. The intervening stretch, normal human
life as we all live it most of the time, was too familiar
to have any magic.

Realism declares that this central stretch of the
normal and the known is in fact where the magic lies.
Needless to say it had to wait for two developments: the
big city and the beginnings of industry. In a big city,
one's next-door neighbour disappears from morning till
night and one has no idea where he is or what he is
doing. If he works in a factory or is employed by a large
company, he himself probably has very little idea of what
he is doing, since his attention is entirely engrossed in
some minute corner of a large enterprise whose total
operation is planned and overseen by people with whom
he has no contact. Both you and he live in a world of the
unknown. The link between you is that you both read the
same newspaper, which picks out of the unfathomable
complexity of the city sudden vivid items, unrelated to
one another, which mainly concern crime, violence,
tragedy or heroism. No wonder the realistic novel grew
up step by step with the newspaper press, and no wonder

so many major realistic novelists began their working lives in newspaper offices.

The growth of the big city produced two strands of realism: one, the attempt to provide some kind of coherent interpretation of the bewilderingly complex urban scene; the other, the political imperative to keep clear of the sentimental illusion and the escapist fantasy. Socialist Realism grows naturally out of the demand for an unremitting series of exposures of unsatisfactory social conditions and the sins of the governing class generally. It is an off-shoot of the notion that art should be primarily a form of propaganda.

Neither of these strands is present in Shakespeare. They were unknown in his world. Nevertheless, I have become convinced, after a decent search for an alternative term, that there are important areas of his work that can only be described as realism, that there is a side of his creativity that is realistic in a true, abiding sense.

II

For an example of how the essential spirit of realism operates in Shakespeare's work, I suggest *The Merchant of Venice*. It interweaves two stories, one centred on Venice, the other on Portia's house at Belmont, and both are, considered simply as stories, totally unconvincing; I suppose that point does not need to be argued. The Belmont plot, with its casket ritual and its finally happy double marriage, is a love-story of the kind that can just about be sustained as long as everything is kept safely within a Nutcracker Suite atmosphere of the fairy-story; the Venice plot, about the pound of flesh, has roots in folk-tale and obviously derives, like the story of Dracula, from some dark and deep level of human phobia. The point of intersection between the two stories, when the disguised Portia defeats Shylock by a silly legal quibble, is merely preposterous, since any reasonable definition of 'flesh' would include the blood that is an essential part of that flesh. The legitimate critical question is, how

21

can Shakespeare, starting with such flimsy materials, achieve a building so solid and memorable?

One explanation, which at first sight has a good deal to be said for it, is that the play is simply a satire on the law, calling into question the whole business of contracts and courts and judges. Certainly law plays a sorry enough role in both stories. In one, a dead father's *Diktat* obliges an intelligent and healthy young woman to stake her chances of a happy marriage on a foolish guessing-game; the further condition, that a suitor who guesses wrong must go away and renounce marriage altogether, not only to Portia but to any woman soever, seems like a mere piece of vindictiveness. As for the tale of Shylock's bond, what it demonstrates is that the law can provide a spurious framework of legitimacy for human beings who, for motives of their own, wish to behave like devils – which means that, in one important respect at least, the two stories are not at all hard to reconcile. The technical business of interweaving plot and sub-plot is carried out very deftly: Portia is released from the oafish tyranny of her dead father not entirely by chance, since we are given to understand that Bassanio has human qualities of perception and understanding of Portia's character, that guide him to the correct choice; after which she, having been set free from one legal noose, rescues Antonio from another again, not by chance but by having certain qualities (quick-wittedness, guile). In this wise, the sympathetic characters are enabled to come through happily despite the monstrous distortions brought about by law. The impression of hostility to the law is strengthened by the fact that Shylock, at the point in the action where he appears as most totally unsympathetic, invokes legality, pointing out that the Christian characters are slave-owners and justify this denial of rights to another human being by pointing to the statute-book:

Duke. How shalt thou hope for mercy, rend'ring none?
Shylock. What judgment shall I dread, doing no wrong?
     You have among you many a purchas'd slave,
     Which, like your asses and your dogs and mules,

You use in abject and in slavish parts,
Because you bought them; shall I say to you
'Let them be free, marry them to your heirs –
Why sweat they under burdens? – let their beds
Be made as soft as yours, and let their palates
Be season'd with such viands'? You will answer
'The slaves are ours'. So do I answer you.

All this adds up to a good satiric case against the law, and yet I can't, in the end, believe that this is what Shakespeare wrote the play to demonstrate. Its richness and power go beyond a mere *exposé* of the law, which, after all, however necessary it may be in the daily business of our lives, has always been recognised by popular wisdom as 'an ass'.

Shylock, obviously, is no mere vehicle for satire. However flimsy the plot in which he figures, he is a totally solid and credible character. There was, of course, an Elizabethan stage convention of the Jew as monster, and in my earliest attempts to get the measure of Shylock's character, as a young student, I began by trying to site him within this tradition. When Antonio's arrival on the scene sends him into soliloquy, almost the opening line of that soliloquy is

I hate him for he is a Christian.

I, at that stage, saw this as relating Shylock to a character like Marlowe's Barabas, a Sweeney Todd type who delights in his own wickedness to the point of tilting the play close to extravagant buffoonery:

Sometimes I go about and poison wells,
And stab sick wretches groaning under walls.

But then I had, in those days, no experience of racial hatred and could not seriously imagine it as a motive. Shylock does, in fact, hate Antonio for being a Christian, and, in view of the way he and his co-religionists are treated by Christians, it would be surprising if he did not. In *Romeo and Juliet* the Montagues and the

Capulets automatically fight when they meet in the street, for no better reason than because that is what they are programmed to do; they have inherited a tradition of conflict which they do not question. In the same way, but with deeper and more tragic historical roots, Christian and Jew in the international trading city of Venice have inherited a situation of conflict, and, in fact, the only character who questions it – or comes somewhere near to questioning it – is Shylock himself.

Shylock brings out the worst in the characters by whom he is surrounded, except for the largely off-stage Tubal. Antonio is shown as the perfect gentleman, the pattern of courtesy and accomplishment; that is how he is regarded in his circle, and no doubt we as the audience are meant to accept that valuation. But Shylock has seen a very different side. When Antonio comes to him for the favour of a loan, he declares himself to be puzzled – legitimately, one would have thought – as to the appropriate reaction.

> Shall I bend low, and in a bondman's key
> With bated breath, and whisp'ring humbleness,
> Say this:
> 'Fair sir, you spit on me on Wednesday last,
> You spurn'd me such a day, another time
> You call'd me dog: and for these courtesies
> I'll lend you thus much moneys'?

Did the gracious, high-bred Antonio whom we see, this 'parfit gentil knight', really treat Shylock with that brutal discourtesy? Certainly; he does not deny it; his answer is that it was the correct thing to do, and nothing is going to stop him doing the correct thing.

> I am as like to call thee so again,
> To spit on thee again, to spurn thee too.
> If thou wilt lend this money, lend it not
> As to thy friends. . . .

The untroubled assumption is that the mere fact of Shylock's not being a Christian is sufficient to put him outside the range of courtesy or charity, and this assumption is common to all the Christian characters in the play, both those we see on stage and those we don't, such as the boys who run after Shylock and mock him in his grief over the loss of daughter and ducats. In the same way, Jessica seems to regard her crossing over from Jew to Christian as a piece of uncomplicated good fortune. It is dramatically credible that she should have no affection for her father, for she has only known his stern side and she sees him as an obstacle to her fulfilment in marriage, but she also feels no pang at all in deserting the whole Hebraic tradition in which she must have been brought up from infancy, and one wonders what the reaction of Shakespeare's audience would have been if the choice had been the other way round, a Christian girl throwing over her religion for love of a Jewish husband.

Jessica is, of course, a mere sketch, a walk-on character in the happy love-story which is, theatrically, the main business of the play. (The light-hearted theatrical movement, of course, is pulling away from the main tide of the play, which is sombre and uncomfortable.) To show her psychology in any detail would have been to introduce complexity at a point where the play could not have supported it; it would have been like digging for motives in the scene where Lancelot Gobbo makes sport of the blindness of his father. In the case of Shylock himself, Shakespeare could not avoid this complexity. The character is too large, and too much in the centre of the stage, to be shown as a cardboard cut-out, no matter how convenient this would have been and no matter how much it might have been the poet's original intention, before his imagination warmed to the work.

Shylock's pathos arises from the fact that he is vulnerable in the area where Jews are traditionally vulnerable: in the strength of his family affections, the closeness of his family ties, his sense of the sacredness of his home and its difference from the homes of those among whom he is a barely tolerated outsider.

Clamber not you up to the casements then

> To gaze on Christian fools with varnish'd faces:
> But stop my house's ears, I mean my casements;
> Let not the sound of shallow fopp'ry enter
> My sober house.

The heart-broken cry of 'I had it of Leah when I was a bachelor; I would not have given it for a wilderness of monkeys' is wrung from his agony at the thought that these spendthrift, unfeeling tormentors have managed to snatch out of his hand, and trample underfoot, something very dear to him, the remembrance of his dead wife.

Equally Jewish is his willingness to dispute. Where the Christian characters are armoured in certainty like a set of Victorian headmasters – their motto might well be Jowett's 'Never apologise, never explain' – he is willing to put the question of usury, ostensibly the chief ground of their hostility, out in the open and talk about it. At the very outset of his conversation with Antonio in I, iii, he brings out the story, from the third chapter of *Genesis*, of Jacob grazing his uncle's sheep, and the means Jacob employed to make sure that a goodly proportion of the season's crop of lambs should be 'party-coloured' (the method used, by the way, is based on exactly the same quirk of mind-and-body interaction which caused Tristram Shandy to be born with an indecisive character, and I have always wondered whether there is anything in the theory or whether it is pure folk-lore). What matters for the play is that Shylock is here taking a step towards the Christian characters, offering to explain Jewish tradition and Jewish attitudes by tracing them back to the sacred writings and thus build a bridge to some kind of understanding. Their response, of course, is to sweep him aside with complacent superiority:

> Mark you this Bassanio:
> The devil can cite Scripture for his purpose, –
> An evil soul producing holy witness
> Is like a villain with a smiling cheek,
> A goodly apple rotten at the heart.
> O what a goodly outside falsehood hath!

The refusal to hear Shylock's side, to concede that it might be possible to learn anything, to gain in understanding in any way, from what he has to say, is total and self-congratulatory. Later (IV, i), when Shylock is having his moment of vindictive ascendancy, Antonio represents him as completely impervious to outside opinion – makes it, indeed, part of his monsterhood that he is so.

> I pray you, think you question with the Jew.
> You may as well go stand upon the beach
> And bid the main flood bate his usual height;
> You may as well use question with the wolf, etc.

The Merchant of Venice, despite the artificiality of its twinned stories, is grounded in a true and solid vision of human nature. The psychology is realistic though the trappings are fanciful, and in aligning the two Shakespeare has so arranged things that the reality, and therefore for my purposes the realism, prevails. Portia's escapade is unconvincing enough at a surface level – it is highly unlikely that a young woman dressed as a man could impose herself as a judge eminent enough to try such an important and urgent case, in the presence of the head of state – but at the level of psychological realism it works out because it fits in with Shakespeare's usual view of the role of the sexes, which is that while men have the capacity to dream dreams and see visions, and occasionally to perform acts of heroism, it is the women who cope with life, manage practical affairs, solve difficulties, keep their heads in a crisis. (Whether I would consider this view 'realistic' if it didn't happen to coincide with my own opinion, I don't know, but it does.) We can pooh-pooh the notion of a girl masquerading as a judge, but not the force of her feminine resourcefulness, which is what the story is really about.

Another feature of the play that makes for realistic solidity is that it is founded on a view of life that is surely borne out by everyone's experience, namely that it is shaped by a combination of two powers: partly by pure chance, and partly by willed action, our own and others'. I take it that no one, looking back on his or her life, would deny that some very important events in it were the result of sheer random accident, impossible to plan for or guard against, and others, equally important, resulted from willed action. So, in this play, Antonio is threatened with an unpleasant death by the willed action of Shylock and saved from it by the willed action of Portia. On the other hand, if the business of the caskets, in which there was certainly some element of the fortuitous, had gone the wrong way, if Portia had been married off to Morocco, it is impossible to imagine him allowing her to go off to Venice on this legal escapade; nor would she have had the motive for it, since an important part of her reason is to please Bassanio and demonstrate the identity of her interests with his. Antonio has put himself into Shylock's power by willed action (agreeing to the bargain), but on the other hand the failure of all his sea-borne enterprises is a most unlikely chance; by assuming that at least some of his ships would get home safely he was taking no more than a calculated risk and would scarcely imagine that chance should go so totally against him. The theme of chance thus becomes an underlying *motif*, common to both plots; when working up his resolve to choose a casket, Morocco says,

> If Hercules and Lichas play at dice
> Which is the better man, the greater throw
> May turn by fortune from the weaker hand.
> So is Alcides beaten by his page;
> And so may I, blind Fortune leading me,
> Miss that which one unworthier may attain,
> And die with grieving.

And Salerio, otherwise a nonentity, has a brilliantly written speech in that conversation with Antonio which opens the play, describing the unquietness in the mind of a merchant whose fortune is at the mercy of the seas.

> My wind, cooling my broth,
> Would blow me to an ague when I thought

What harm a wind too great might do at sea.
I should not see the sandy hour-glass run
But I should think of shallows and of flats,
And see my wealthy Andrew dock'd in sand,
Vailing her high top lower than her ribs
To kiss her burial. Should I go to church
And see the holy edifice of stone,
And not bethink me straight of dangerous gales,
Which, touching but my gentle vessel's side,
Would scatter all her spices on the stream,
Enrobe the roaring waters with my silks,
And, in a word, but even now worth this,
And now worth nothing? Shall I have the
     thought
To think on this, and shall I lack the thought
That such a thing bechanc'd would make me
     sad?

In these lines we can see Shakespeare's imagination delighting in its own power; the writing is wonderful; a line like

Enrobe the roaring waters with my silks

says so much in ten syllables that we can hardly unpack it. In its fullness of sound it approaches 'imitative form', i.e. we can hear the surge of the ocean in the sound of the words. Then there is that flavour of the extravagant, even that touch of the surreal, that seems never to be far from Shakespeare's poetic mind. (It has always struck me as strange that though understatement is such a natural mode of expression in England, and so much in English literature gets its effects by understatement, the national poet should be a poet of hyperbole.) Over it all is the dominant impression – all-conquering nature versus puny man. Shakespeare's work is full of images of this theme; writing at a time when man's challenge to nature was just beginning to be mounted, when *homo sapiens* was building more elaborate contrivances and bigger cities, when the scientific revolution was only just round the corner and indeed, in the mind of a man like

Bacon, had already started, Shakespeare continually presents as *hubris* the notion that man can treat nature as an underling; as when Apemantus demands of Timon,

> What, think'st
> That the bleak air, thy boisterous chamberlain,
> Will put thy shirt on warm?

But Salerio's speech, for all its dazzling early-Shake-spearean brilliance, merely demonstrates a predictable misunderstanding; it does not reach out to what Antonio actually has in his mind. The reason for his melancholy is nothing to do with his mercantile risks, which he is inured to living with; it arises from the fact that, his sexual emotions being of that particular nature, he loves Bassanio and knows that he must shortly lose him to a woman. Later, under the pressures that build up in the course of the action, Antonio makes a movingly direct statement of these inner feelings when he says that, since his problems are in any case insoluble, he might as well resign himself to death and regard it as, in its own way, a blessing.

> I am a tainted wether of the flock,
> Meetest for death; the weakest kind of fruit
> Drops earliest to the ground, and so let me.
> You cannot better be employ'd, Bassanio,
> Than to live still, and write mine epitaph.

III

Shakespeare's work is very often concerned with politics, i.e. with the question of who gets hold of the power and what they do with it when they have got it. His other two themes are (i) what are now called 'interpersonal relationships', the reaction of one human being to another, and (ii) metaphysical, the reaction of the human being to the ageless questions of the nature of the universe and what we are supposed to be doing in it. In a very large-scale play like *Hamlet*, these three themes are given about equal weight; in an overtly political play like *Julius Caesar*, the other two themes, though sketched in with a master's hand, are subordinate to questions of power. And there is hardly a play in the canon that could be said to contain no politics at all. This can be illustrated by going back briefly to *The Merchant of Venice*. As a rule Shakespeare's settings are purely notional and do not seem to mean much to him in themselves, but he evidently had a clear idea of Venice, not only as the most important and splendid of the Italian city-states ('This is Venice,' says Brabantio to Iago, 'my house is not a grange') and also as a place that earned its wealth by international trade, something that would be clear to a man like Shakespeare who was for twenty years a Londoner. When the assembled dignitaries use all their persuasive force on Shylock, before Portia succeeds in turning the trick, to get him to relent and cancel his bond, his answer is that a legal agreement is a legal agreement, and if they refuse to honour it he will see that the international trading community hears that Venice is no longer a place where a man can strike a secure bargain. This, as he knows, is an argument against which they have no defence; it strikes at the roots of their state; it reminds one of that passage in Magna Carta insisting above all on safe conduct for merchants. Politics is the art of the possible, and Shakespeare always kept a clear eye on that art.

The scrutiny of political themes and political motives in Shakespeare is 'realistic' in the sense that it is shrewd, penetrating, pragmatic. The poet is not optimistic, neither does he allow his vision to become blurred by facile pessimism. He sees things as they are.

Some people have found that the most non-realistic or anti-realistic feature of Shakespeare's political drama is his heavy exploitation, in the English historical plays, of the notion of the Divine Right of Kings, which William Empson dismissed as 'a pompous myth made up to flatter the Tudors'. In fact, of course, like every political myth which had a hope of succeeding in the sixteenth century, it rested on a Scriptural foundation; in the Third Book of Kings 9. 1–5, the Lord makes an agreement with

Solomon. Biblical or not, however, is not the doctrine highly unrealistic, in a world of *Realpolitik*?

The answer is that it would be if human beings were rational, but they are nothing of the sort. A quick way to indicate what I mean is to refer to George Orwell's short, incisive essay 'Wells, Hitler, and the World State' (1941). H. G. Wells had grown up at a time when it seemed that the rationality of Victorian science would sweep away religion, superstition, the tradition of acceptance of social injustice, and with them mumbo-jumbo of every sort. He had advocated a reasonable, hedonistic view of life and politics in which outrages like war would automatically be rejected because people would be too sensible to go in for them. In fact, as Orwell points out, Wells is growing old in a world dominated by nightmare figures like Hitler, whose appeal is to the dark gods, to blood, sorrow and sacrifice in pursuit of some mystical doctrine of a Master-Race. Hitler's notions were a tissue of rubbish, Wells's were eminently sensible, but it was Hitler who had a powerful nation behind him. 'Hitler is a criminal lunatic,' Orwell wrote, 'and Hitler has an army of millions of men, aeroplanes in thousands, tanks in tens of thousands. For his sake a great nation has been willing to over-work itself for six years and then to fight for two years more, whereas for the common-sense, essentially hedonistic world-view which Mr Wells puts forward, hardly a human creature is willing to shed a pint of blood.' And he goes on to note that the will to stand up to German military power arose in the British not because of any national enlightenment, but from 'the atavistic emotion of patriotism, the ingrained feeling of the English-speaking peoples that they are superior to foreigners'.

Without suggesting that the doctrine of Divine Right is necessarily one that would be held by 'a criminal lunatic', I hope my point is clear: the theory is a way of enlisting a sanction, a supra-rational mystique, into the day-to-day business of governing and of putting down rebellions. Shakespeare was born into what was still recognisably a feudal society, though it was beginning here and there to give way before that combination of mass democracy and straight plutocracy that we have today. In a feudal society there are a number of heavily armed barons, each with a private army. One of them has the title of King, and just about the only advantage he has over his rivals is that he does have that title. There can be no stability in the realm – and Shakespeare passionately desired and eloquently advocated stability – unless people in general can be made to feel that to dethrone the anointed king, however expedient, is *wrong*. He also saw, I believe, that there is no way of persuading them of this by mere argumentation; you have to appeal to their primitive, irrational – what Orwell calls 'atavistic' – emotions.

The English historical plays, then, are based on an acceptance of the doctrine of Divine Right, and the cases in which that acceptance has to be suspended – the cases of both the Richards – are special cases bristling with problems which it is the business of the plays to solve. And needless to say Shakespeare did not accept the doctrine with open-mouthed simplicity. The most succinct statement of it anywhere in his work –

Let him go, Gertrude.
There's such divinity doth hedge a king
That treason doth but peep to what it would,
Acts little of his will

– is uttered by a crowned man who has murdered a king before the action opens and will himself be killed before it ends.

The particular interest of the Roman plays, on the other hand, is that, since their setting is pre-Christian and their political tradition remote from that of England, Shakespeare could come at these political problems directly, without having to begin from the position of accepting Divine Right. This freed his hands considerably, and I believe there is an eagerness, a willingness to take full advantage of what the Roman theme offered him, in the fact that the three plays deal with three completely different facets of Roman history: the early Republic in *Coriolanus*, the zenith of empire in *Julius*

Caesar, and, in *Antony and Cleopatra,* the same period but seen from the perspective, not of Rome, but of the far-flung Empire. Each play thrashes out complex matters of leadership, illustrating those qualities that bring men to mastery and then put them on the block. The Coriolanus whose self-forgetful pursuit of honour makes him, briefly, the idol of the populace is the same whose patrician code leads him to sacrifice himself to a mother's plea and go back to face a lynch-mob. The Antony whose passionate, outgoing spirit enables him to mobilise that same mob against the cabal who killed Caesar is the same who cannot resist the enervating magic of Cleopatra. Julius Caesar is destroyed by the antagonism of an *élite,* whose motives range from envy, in the case of Cassius, to high-minded worries about despotism, in the case of Brutus. All the plays are instinct with political awareness, and the manipulation of power is seen in its relationship to character, just as it is in the case of Henry the Fifth, or, for that matter, Claudius. Thus at one end of the spectrum we have the tribunes, who must catch at power by exploiting every gust of popular sentiment and trimming their sails to it; at the other end, a character like Volumnia, whose advice to her son is a superb dramatic encapsulation of the attitude of the conservative aristocratic politician:

Coriolanus Why did you wish me milder? Would you
              have me
              False to my nature? Rather say I play
              The man I am.
Volumnia   O! sir, sir, sir,
              I would have had you put your power well
              on
              Before you had worn it out. . . .
              If it be honour in your wars to seem
              The same you are not, which for your best
              ends
              You adopt your policy, how is it less or
              worse
              That it shall hold companionship in peace

34

	With honour as in war; since that to both
	It stands in like request?
Coriolanus	Why force you this?
Volumnia	Because that now it lies you on to speak

        To th' people, not by your own instruction,
        Nor by th' matter which your heart prompts you,
        But with such words that are but rooted in
        Your tongue, though but bastards and syllables
        Of no allowance to your bosom's truth.
        Now, this no more dishonours you at all
        Than to take in a town with gentle words,
        Which else would put you to your fortune and
        The hazard of much blood.
        I would dissemble with my nature where
        My fortunes and my friends at stake requir'd
        I should do so in honour. I am in this
        Your wife, your son, these senators, the nobles;
        And you will rather show our general louts
        How you can frown, than spend a fawn upon 'em
        For the inheritance of their loves and safeguard
        Of what that want might ruin.

This kind of writing is political realism at its most incisive, not laid out in blocks as in the 19th-century play of ideas, but fully integrated in the study of human character; the personages hold the ideas they hold because they are the people they are, and then the ideas breed within them and end by distorting their personhood.

IV

Shakespeare's double plots are also a vehicle for his realism. They tend to mitigate the dream-quality of his settings, if only because, whatever the hypothetical scene of the action, there is an unstated but unbreakable convention that whenever the comic characters enter, the scene effectively changes to England. *Much Ado* is supposed to happen in Messina, but Dogberry, Verges and their colleagues are the town watch of Stratford, just as Autolycus, in 'Bohemia', is an English pedlar.

Shakespeare is so deeply English that his imagery is habitually rural and Cotswold, whether or not this would be particularly appropriate to the speaker. Enobarbus, seeking for words contemptuous enough to describe Cleopatra's hasty retreat from the battle of Actium (she hadn't enough self-knowledge to foresee that she would be frightened when the fighting started) says savagely,

> Yon ribaudred nag of Egypt –
> Whom leprosy o'ertake! – i' th' midst o' th' fight,
> When vantage like a pair of twins appear'd
> Both as the same, or rather ours the elder –
> The breese upon her, like a cow in June,
> Hoists sails and flies.

The sails of Cleopatra's boat did indeed fill with the 'breeze' in the sense of wind, and it is hard (and perhaps unnecessary) to keep that association out, but Enobarbus is using 'breese' (or 'breeze') in the sense of 'gadfly.' Sometimes, in June, one sees a cluster of cows standing quietly together, and all of a sudden one starts to run, impelled by the painful little jab of the gadfly. The image perfectly conveys what Enobarbus feels about Cleopatra, but it is an image from Warwickshire, not from Egypt. It shows that typical Shakespearean blend of a realism that makes the characters talk in concrete, observed metaphor and the larger unrealism that distributes these metaphors among the characters without caring much for likelihood. Iago wants Othello to draw his sword and resist the search-party led by Brabantio, because that will embroil him still further and make his situation worse, but Othello answers, in a metaphor drawn not from his own *métier* but from Shakespeare's,

> Were it my cue to fight, I should have known it
> Without a prompter.

If we postulate the existence of Othello as a real person, the likelihood is that in his wandering life of camps and bivouacs he had never seen a theatre, but the image of the prompter is natural to Shakespeare the actor and theatre shareholder, so he makes it natural for Othello, too. Perdita, the strayed princess brought up by cottagers, is unlikely to know much about the manufacture of books, but Shakespeare was familiar with the printing-house and the bookstall, so he has Perdita say to Florizel, in her anxiety about what his royal father will say to their match,

> Even now I tremble
> To think your father, by some accident,
> Should pass this way, as you did. O, the Fates!
> How would he look to see his work, so noble,
> Vilely bound up?

All this might be described as displaced realism. The homely, vivid images are sharp and precise; within the range of Shakespeare's poetry they counterbalance the effect of a line like 'Enrobe the roaring waters with my silks,' which is a product of the apocalyptic imagination. That he distributes them at random among characters who would not in actuality have been likely to use them gives a flickering quality to the realism with which his language is permeated. And this is where we must sound a caution. Realism of psychology, realism of political analysis, we can all recognise – provided only that we have enough experience of life to know these things when we encounter them. But what exactly constitutes realism in Shakespeare's language when it is fully lit by imagination – i.e. in the passages of either lofty poetry or extravagant humour – is an area where we must tread carefully. To make my point clear I must conclude with an example of Getting It Wrong: not in any point-scoring spirit, for in such a rich and complex field as Shakespearean commentary we can all make mistakes, but to illustrate the kind of care that is needed. I refer to *Much Ado About Nothing*, V, i, in the New Cambridge edition (1962). Dogberry and his fellows have discharged their role in the action by revealing Don John's plot to disgrace Hero and abort the wedding; Borachio has confessed; Dogberry and Verges confront Leonato, in the hall of his great house, their duty over, and receive his gracious tribute:

> I thank thee for thy care and honest pains.

Dogberry, who knows that his cue is to go away, has no idea how to do it; the etiquette of leaving a great person's presence is too much for him; he burbles on for a few lines; Leonato gives him a purse of money.

> *Leonato:* There's for thy pains.
> *Dogberry:* God save the foundation!

Dogberry still cannot go. It is quite clear how this scene should be played. Dogberry, gripping the senile Verges by the wrist, is inching backwards out of the presence. Leonato again utters a sentence which contains the imperative 'Go.' Dogberry is slithering backwards to the accompaniment of a steady fountain of pish-posh, made up of the wreckage of what his confused mind brings up as courteous phrases, fitted for converse with the high-born.

> – Go, I discharge thee of thy prisoner, and I thank thee.
> – I leave an arrant knave with your worship, which I beseech your worship to correct yourself, for the example of others. God keep your worship, I wish your worship well, God restore you to health, I humbly give you leave to depart

– and if a merry meeting may be wished, God
prohibit it. Come neighbour.

He is stuffed to bursting with feelings of pride, awe,
self-importance, and plain embarrassment, and keeps up
a steady fire of these broken phrases until, judging the
door to be close behind him, he suddenly turns and bolts
out, dragging the stupefied Verges with that last yelp of
'Come neighbour.' It is an irresistibly comic scene, a rare
example of a character making a complete fool of himself
without arousing in us any contempt, only indulgent
laughter. There seems nothing much to comment on, and
indeed my comment is not on Shakespeare but on his
commentators, in this case the Cambridge editors
(Quiller-Couch and Dover Wilson). On the line 'God save
the foundation!' uttered by Dogberry when he receives
a present of money, they begin by pointing out, with
acknowledgement to Steevens, that this was 'the
customary phrase employed by those who received alms
at the gates of religious houses'. On this, they get to
work.

Commentators seem to have missed the humour of
this. The pressure of the coin on his palm brings the
accustomed patter to Dogberry's lips, and shows how 'one
that hath two shirts, and everything handsome about
him' actually maintained himself. It is a finishing touch.

To say that other people have 'missed the humour' of
something, when oneself failing to see a joke, is an old
pitfall and we can be sympathetic. But over-literalness
of this kind has no place in the interpretation of Shakespeare. Dogberry's speech is full of phrases half-remem-
bered from 'accustomed patter' of one kind and another.
When he is given money, he vaguely remembers that
the correct thing to say is 'God save the foundation', so
he says it. To adduce this solemnly as proof that he is a
professional mendicant who spends his life hanging
about religious houses (a perfectly possible *métier* in the
16th century in Southern Europe but hardly in England
after the Reformation, if we are going to look for
'realism') is to get Dogberry totally wrong. I see him, as
surely we are meant to, as a respectable tradesman;

bumbling, inarticulate, but respectable; I believe that he had two shirts and everything handsome about him; I even believe that he had 'had losses'.

The learned Cambridge editors took this phrase of Dogberry's as realistic in a heavily literal sense, as bearing down directly on the supposed biography of the character who utters it. Let that serve as a warning to us. Shakespeare is a realistic writer, but not always and everywhere, and not always in the same way.

On Your Imaginary Forces Work

BRAHAM MURRAY

From the age of eight to the age of thirteen I attended a Berkshire Prep School straight out of the pages of Waugh's *Decline and Fall*. The English Master was a Mr Robertson, better known as Willie Fluff because he had an abundance of fluffy blond hair at the sides of a balding pate. Willie Fluff was nicotine–stained at every conceivable point: from his fingertips to his elbows, from his teeth to the whites of his eyes. He was an eccentric. His greatest eccentricity was his passionate love for *Macbeth* which he knew off by heart and used to act out to us when we should have been learning the basics of English Grammar. He acted it out with such verve and gusto and with such total involvement in all the characters from Macbeth himself through the witches (especially the witches) to the assorted Lords, that I was totally transported by him into the world of the play. What a world it was! Ghosts, apparitions, witches, battles, feasts, murders crowded in, one on top of the other, and at the same time the story of Macbeth was so clear that you followed his fate with the sympathy that he should command, in spite of his wrongdoings. What I did not know then was how many directors and actors had tried to achieve just that and failed. Willie Fluff knew each of the characters intimately as if they were his friends. He conjured them up uninhibitedly. There was none of the awful weight of interpreting a cultural giant hampering him. His was a healthy relationship with Shakespeare. What is more, I understood the play in spite of my bare ten years and in spite of the fact that I had never come into contact with Shakespeare in any other shape or form. Later on, at Public School and at Oxford, I was taught by first–rate teachers and tutors, but I believe to this day that Willie Fluff was the most important English Teacher I ever had.

The above is not mere sentimental reminiscence. I know from having talked to many teachers how difficult Shakespeare is to teach. Indeed, some have told me that, given the option of not teaching it at 'O' level, they grab it. I also know the difficulties of directing Shakespeare for the theatre. The single fact is that people of all ages, for various reasons, have a block about Shakespeare. I have never had that block, thanks to Willie Fluff. Once you have encountered Shakespeare in good circumstances you can survive endless bad productions (even the BBC complete works!) and dreadful teaching.

What I hope to do in this essay is to try to explain what processes a director goes through when preparing a production, first in the analysis and design stage and then in rehearsal. I shall refer a lot to productions I have done, not out of egoism, but because I know them best, and especially a recent production of *Hamlet* with Robert Lindsay, which was seen at the Royal Exchange Theatre, Manchester, on tour around the country, and finally at the Barbican during the latter part of '83 and the beginning of '84. I shall do this because there are such obvious parallels between introducing students to Shakespeare and trying to inspire a new company of actors, and because Shakespeare wrote for the theatre; he wrote for his plays to be performed, and the twang of backstage somehow takes the curse off the overly academic approach. If, in the following pages, you substitute the word 'teacher' for director, you might be surprised at how similar our roles are or, dare I say it, 'should be'. It is to be hoped that reading how a director approaches rehearsals may start some new ideas in you as to how such approaches could be adapted for the classroom.

An actor once told me that he worked in the theatre in order to try and 'illuminate the darkness' for the audience. That expresses perfectly why I direct plays. The theatre is a place where people gather to share with another group of people (called actors) a journey of some three hours' duration in the course of which they will examine the mysteries of existence which apply to each and every one of us. Hopefully they will leave the theatre a little strengthened, a little refreshed, a little illuminated.

I know of no serious theatre practitioner who does not regard Shakespeare as the acid test of his capabilities. This is because, in the spectrum of his work, Shakespeare examines all of the great questions of our existence, be they personal, political or spiritual, and brings to them such a breadth of perception, such a richness of understanding that when he expresses them through his incomparable artistic skills we glimpse the light, even if it be but dimly lit.

This rather general paragraph leads me to the first crucial point. Before he can expect to be able to inspire actors, designers, composers etc., etc., the director must establish within himself a genuinely personal relationship with the play he is to direct. If you can make a play alive to yourself then you have a chance of directing it well; if not, all the expertise won't save you, even if you objectively admire it very much. It is no use doing *Hamlet* just because it's a 'great' play and every director wants to 'do' it in his career. The teacher doing *A Midsummer Night's Dream* for the umpteenth time, because it is on the 'O' level syllabus, is in an even more dangerous situation. Just as I often go to a distinguished, and preferably controversial, academic to get my processes sharpened up, so I would suggest a visit to one or more productions in the theatre. Failing that, seeking out an actor or director associated with an interesting production of the play might help to make the teacher re-approach the text from a fresh angle. It is astonishing how a Shakespearean text will yield more and more riches if your relationship with it is constantly renewed.

I wanted to direct *Hamlet* as soon as I became a

director. I set up two different productions which never came to fruition (thankfully, in retrospect) until in 1979 I did a production of *The Lower Depths* with Bob Lindsay. He seemed to me a brilliant young actor who, without trying, spoke directly to a modern audience; they instinctively understood that he was one of them. I asked him if he would be interested in playing Hamlet and he was excited by the idea. I put the project up to my colleagues and they asked me why I wanted to do *Hamlet*. It was a simple question but it floored me completely! Why did I indeed? I went back and read the text again. What story was it telling? Was it a story I wanted to tell? Was it a story I could tell? Three crucial questions that every director should ask himself.

I read it extremely carefully and came immediately to the conclusion that it was, in fact, a silly play about an inadequate young man who, through abject vacillation, managed to get everything wrong and ended up dead. That wasn't a story I wanted to tell. I dismissed the project from my mind – at which point, of course, it began to work on me and in me.

> O God, Horatio, what a wounded name,
> Things standing thus unknown, shall I leave
>   behind me.
> If thou did'st ever hold me in thy heart,
> Absent thee from felicity awhile,
> And in this harsh world draw thy breath in pain
> To tell my story.

Hamlet knew much better than I did about his own failure. He also knew that the story of his failure might just inspire other people wrestling with the same problem to continue the struggle, perhaps more successfully than he was able to do. Horatio would validate his life by telling his story.

Shakespeare begins his story of Hamlet at that poignant moment when the scales of childhood fall from our eyes. We see the world as it exists. Our parents are not the faultless demi-gods we believed them to be, the men who govern us are not the super–intellectual, selfless paragons of virtue that they seemed, the police are not the reliable guardians of our safety we thought them; and over all this looms puberty, releasing in us titanic forces that sometimes seem to run at odds with every other part of our being. This overwhelming experience is one of the most crucial of our lives. Our ability to cope with this affects the rest of our lives. Hamlet's initial reaction to the challenge is marvellously expressed:

> O that this too too sullied flesh would melt,
> Thaw and resolve itself into a dew,
> Or that the Everlasting had not fix'd
> His canon 'gainst self-slaughter. O God! O God!
> How weary, stale, flat and unprofitable
> Seem to me all the uses of this world!

What young person of sensitivity has not felt that, and how many have uttered the equivalent of those fateful and sometimes fatal words:

> The time is out of joint. O cursèd spite,
> That ever I was born to set it right.

In that couplet, I felt, lay the essence of the tragedy. The business of a man is to put himself right, then he can turn outwards. If he does not put himself right he will project the poison of his own unresolved side into the situation. This is Hamlet's error and he pays for it with his life. By the end of the play, Hamlet has reached a cosmic peacefulness in himself.

> There's a special providence in the fall of a
> sparrow. If it be now, 'tis not to come; if it be
> not to come, it will be now; if it be not now, yet
> it will come: the readiness is all.

It is too late for his life but not for ours. Yes, this was a play I wanted to do. I knew that I could now make vital Hamlet's affair with Ophelia, dislike of Polonius, relationship with his two fathers, and friendships, betrayed or confirmed, with Horatio, Laertes, Rosencrantz and Guildenstern. I knew I could ask Bob to speak with the voice of now, expressing dissatisfaction with our society, battling to right it and failing to realise, as so many fail to do, that society is only an outward expression of people's inner natures.

I cannot emphasise too much that this establishing of a personal relationship with the text is the first step. A director, on the first day of rehearsal, has to make a speech to a group of insecure actors who are probably terrified of Shakespeare. In that speech he must connect them to the core of the play, genuinely. They must know why they are doing that seventeenth–century play in 1985 and just how important it is. I isolate the themes of the play and quote from the newspapers, the modern equivalent. A class in school could do this for themselves. It might be difficult at first and perhaps a bit obvious, i.e. Richard Nixon/Macbeth ... or the Shah of Persia/ Richard II, but gradually they would begin to refine the process until they would identify characters with people they know, recognise traits like Benedick's attitude to women and finally see how the play bears on the problems in their everyday lives. If you can get them to do that you have probably won your most important victory.

You will have fired their enthusiasm enough to give them the energy to attack the biggest difficulty with Shakespeare for a newcomer: the language. The director in his study must understand every word of the text. He must be very careful that his academic preparation is thorough. He must be able very quickly to explain the most obscure passages to the actors, so they don't get bogged down in the way that many of us do when faced with a page of algebra! A talented actor is not necessarily a good academic! The director will then have to convince the actor that the impact of the poetry as part of the dramatic acting is so great that it transcends any obscurity that the language has for the audience. The director must love the shape and form of the dramatic poetry:

O all you host of heaven! O earth! What else?

46

And shall I couple hell? O fie! Hold, hold, my heart,
And you, my sinews, grow not instant old,
But bear me stiffly up.

Shakespeare conveys the feeling of a man bursting at
the seams both inwardly and outwardly. The director
must know that the caesuras (two in the first line, two
in the second, two in the third, and a half-line to end the
thought) will help the actor achieve that heart-
thumping, lung-bursting state that demands to be
expressed through the cosmic imagery.

One thing the director does in the study, that the
teacher can't do, is to cut the text. The director can excise
any 'dead wood' that there might be. In *Hamlet* the text
was pared down to about 2 hours 50 minutes. The cuts
were made in relation to the decision to make it a
domestic Hamlet so that seventeenth–century politics
were excised from it. It might be a healthy exercise for
teachers to ask their classes what they might cut from
a text and to justify the cut. It would be a reminder that
they are reading a text to be played in the theatre. In
order to cut the text however, the academic work has to
be thorough. But what seems a dull prospect becomes as
exciting as a detective story when it has a production as
its justification. With *Hamlet* it became clear to me that
no one knows what the real text of *Hamlet* is. The Folio
and the Quarto differ in crucial aspects; for instance,
'How all occasions . . .' does not appear in the Folio.
Most excitingly, the so-called Bad Quarto, apart from its
deficiencies, has an order of scenes which places 'To be
or not to be' much earlier, and does not split the two
players' scenes. It's an order that seemed to Bob Lindsay
and me to work much better for Hamlet emotionally, so,
because the Bad Quarto seemed to be an actors' text and
so quite possibly represented performance revision, we
adopted its order. More controversially, I decided to cut
Fortinbras, because the entrance of a character called
literally Strong-In-Arms at the end of the play, as a
symbol of hope for the future, seemed, in modern terms,
unplayable. It threatened to spoil Shakespeare's main
theme: that here was a special soul who had tried and

failed to solve some of the great mysteries of life but who might, by his example, help us to do better. The important thing is that none of these decisions could be taken without a good deal of academic preparation, but preparation which was in itself exciting, because it had an objective.

There is another barrier, to theatregoers and students alike, to the enjoyment of Shakespeare and that lies in the sets and costumes that help to sprinkle a layer of dust over his work. Shakespearean production tends to make the plays look like museum pieces. The Elizabethan doublet and hose distances the experience from the audience; it all seems to take place in another world which is nothing to do with our own. The actors strut and posture like creatures from another planet and a glazed look of polite cultural boredom settles on the spectators' features. I have wrestled with the problem for years. I have done an Elizabethan *Merchant,* a non-period, all-purpose, crypto-mediaeval-robed *Winter's Tale,* a Napoleonic *Much Ado*, an authentic period *Macbeth* and a modern-dress *Measure*. The authentic period production was like the Elizabethan; moving the period just created extra problems (a seventeenth-century play, set in the nineteenth-century, in a twentieth-century production) and the modern-dress *Measure* kept the audience in a state of 'Ooh, isn't that clever!' and the critics in a state of pigeonholing and labelling: the play was nowhere.

When I approached *Hamlet* the problem loomed large again. You must have memories of that first scene. The curtain goes up. There are cut-out battlements against a lit cyclorama, the wind whistles mournfully, and there are three actors in funny helmets brandishing pikes doing 'It's late, cold and I can't see' acting. Then the ghost appears. The audience knows it isn't a ghost and are simply interested in how clever the director has been. The scene does not come alive, consequently the play gets off to a dull start. Ten minutes later, the members of court appear in their robes and crowns, and there is a chair and in it the black figure of the prince. I couldn't bear the idea of all that. I wanted the play to be as immediate and urgent to the audience as it was to me. What to do?

I went back to what I knew of Shakespeare's own methods. At the Globe, *Hamlet* would have been played in broad daylight and virtually without scenery. The text itself contained all the audience needed to know about time and place and the actors would take them on the imaginative trip into suspending disbelief. What an exciting idea! I dispensed with scenery. The audience came into a bare theatre (the Royal Exchange is theatre-in-the-round) and when the play started bright lights flooded the stage area. We were saying to the audience 'Don't watch us! Be with us'. The actors sat with the audience on the front row and got up or sat down to make their entrances and exits. This broke down the audience/actor barrier even further and introduced an element of excitement into the proceedings. You never knew who you were sitting next to! That was how the ghost appeared. An actor got up and the actors on-stage reacted to him *as if* he were a ghost, consequently the audience played the same game. Their imagination was actively involved.

The costumes were a greater problem. Going back to Shakespeare's theatre again, I found that all his plays were performed in contemporary Elizabethan costume. It didn't matter if you were a Roman, a Greek or a Barbarian, whether you were an ancient Briton, a Scottish king or a Blackamoor, you appeared in what was, to an Elizabethan audience, modern dress. I tried to apply this to *Hamlet* and it failed from the word go. How do you put a King into modern dress? Kings mean very little to us now. The Shah of Persia was the nearest image I could find: not very useful. My solution was to attempt to extend the style of the settings by having the actors in no costumes at all! They played the play in their street clothes and the audience were asked to imagine armour, or nightdress, or whatever was necessary. Actually, the street clothes were carefully designed in order not to hinder the play: it would have been very unhelpful if Ophelia had arrived at the theatre one night in a sexy dress, for example! The result was that the actors came from the same world as the audience. For young people, especially, the fact that Hamlet was a bit scruffy, uncaring as to whether he had brushed his hair or not, wearing the kind of clothes they wore, was crucial to the success of the play.

On the day of the public dress rehearsal I was nervously pacing around the theatre, waiting for the second half to begin, when I heard a woman say 'It's the first time I've ever understood Shakespeare. I think it's because they haven't got all those costumes. It makes you listen instead.'

She had, to my relief, hit the nail on the head. The audience, with nothing to distract them, after the initial shock, actually listened to the text and the actors, with no scenery and no beards to hide behind, played with great intensity and truthfulness. The play *was* the thing! Just to point up the style, when the Players arrived they came from the old-fashioned theatre, with all the props and costumes and effects and music that we had rigorously excluded.

This whole exercise was designed to make the characters as accessible as any modern play. It was just as important for the actors as for the audience. When Hamlet met Rosencrantz and Guildenstern for the first time they could actually act like old schoolboy friends. The style of playing was relaxed and informal. It was as of now. I must emphasise, however, that the most rigorous standards were applied to the speaking of the verse, and the characterisation was not tampered with to give the play a 'modern' angle. I would have thought that it would be helpful for students to imagine productions, especially to conceive what the characters should look like. Shakespeare intended his plays to be contemporary; we must respect his wishes.

What I want to do now is to take one scene, the encounter between Hamlet and the Ghost, and try to explain how we can make it work. First, I should explain that Claudius and the Ghost were played by the same actor. This underlined one of Hamlet's central dilemmas. To him Old Hamlet was perfect, and Claudius (his other father) the incarnation of evil. In fact one's father is a mixture; to believe him perfect is very dangerous. This approach of having the same actor play both parts made the final death of Claudius especially moving: Hamlet had killed his father.

We were determined that the scene would be about father and son. The absence of ghostly effects helped this. When Hamlet turned, on 'Look my Lord, it comes', he saw his father, 'daddy'. There was a long pause then he asked genuinely 'Angels and ministers of grace defend us!' He knew that his father was dead and that he must be careful, this could be a vision from hell. But then 'I'll call thee Hamlet, King, father, Royal Dane' was almost too much for him: son to father. Then he asked, as we would do:

> But tell
> Why thy canonised bones, hearsed in death
> Have burst their cerements; why the sepulchre,
> Wherein we saw thee quietly interred
> Hath oped his ponderous and marble jaws
> To cast thee up again!

and he asked it exactly as a man who had seen his dearly beloved father buried would ask it, full of love and mystery and dread. He threw off the warnings of his best friend because his love for his father was so great that he could not not follow him. Then, when they were finally alone, the ghost spoke, not as a ghost from a horror movie but as a loving father, and when he said:

> My hour is almost come,
> When I to sulphurous and tormenting flames
> Must render up myself.

his son's rejoinder, 'Alas, poor ghost!', was almost unbearable. Then came the shock. The purpose of the father, consumed with bitterness and hatred, was to poison the son's mind and incite him to revenge, murderous and bloody, to perpetuate the chain of violence. Having softened up his son, having opened up his love, 'If thou did'st ever thy dear father love', he demands and extracts his son's oath to 'Revenge his foul and most unnatural murder.' In this production he reduced Hamlet to pulp with his graphic description of the murder and the mother's infidelity. They were not long 'Shakespearean' lists, but specific, awful images which left Hamlet practically vomiting at his feet. You could see that because Hamlet had such an idealised vision of his father he allowed the poison to enter into him without any realisation of its inherent evil. The final 'Remember me' was not a weak fading-away ghostly invocation, but a searing demanding threat, and when it was reiterated in the following scene from beneath the earth it had the same unforgettable tone of command. You knew just what this father/son relationship was.

In Sheridan Le Fanu's Ghost Stories, ghosts appear without any otherworldly accretions. This is really frightening: a person you know to be dead suddenly appearing quite normally in front of you. This is what happened here, and one of the two central relationships of Hamlet's life was made vivid. I have never seen this scene played as between Father and Son; we are usually too busy with sepulchral tones and clever effects. This was one of the most dramatic examples of a familiar, famous scene coming alive, and it set a standard for the other scenes. Every image had to be made to work in a personal and dramatic way and if we couldn't make it work we went on until we could. It is surprising how, if the actor knows what the line means and plays it with truth, the line will work on the audience even if its language is obscure:

> Cut off even in the blossoms of my sin,
> Unhouseled, disappointed, unaneled.

poses no problem. The sound of the words reaches beyond the brain to the heart, if the actor is doing his job. I am sure it would benefit a class immeasurably if a teacher were to encourage pupils to produce a scene or scenes. It would require a great deal of preparatory work on the part of the teacher so that the pupils could be nursed to the point where they could make contact with the people they were playing, and conceive them, with their clothes and in their environment, but once this was achieved it would inform their approach to the rest of the text in class. Some teachers might find this task a bit daunting. I would suggest trying to get actors from a local theatre to come and talk about a scene or work with the students. I remember an electrifying talk that Judi Dench gave on playing Juliet. I was doing 'A' level, and it made me realise that Juliet was a young, hot-blooded, sexy girl, *not* the stuffy, removed creature that seemed to be in my teacher's mind. Thereafter the play was easy to study. Yes, they wanted to go to bed together, just like you or me! If you can't get actors to come, and you'd be surprised how easy it is, take the class to see a production of the play. As a last resort, get one of those dreary BBC tapes, but be prepared to tear it to pieces.

You must make the audience care about each person as much as a television audience cares about the characters in *Crossroads*. There are immense difficulties in *Hamlet*. Take, for example, Laertes. While Hamlet is in England, Laertes becomes the focal point for a crucial half hour later on in the play, and then must fight a duel with Hamlet and die so that his death has meaning – and yet he only has one really substantial scene at the beginning of the play to make us care about him. That scene is an important one, and, once again, so well known that it is difficult to make vivid. It is important to take seriously the Polonius family, very tight-knit, very fond of each other. Very wretched at the prospect of Laertes going. Laertes has eventually to be almost thrown out by his father. Polonius's advice to Laertes must not be played as if by a buffoon; Laertes must be genuinely moved by it.

> This above all: to thine own self be true
> And it must follow, as the night the day,
> Thou can'st not then be false to any man.

Laertes' advice to Ophelia is not that of a young prig, but of a loving brother, knowing from his own experience how dangerous these sexual matters are and how embarrassing it is to talk about such things to your own sister. If you mine this scene for its family content you will find immense subtlety and warmth in the family relationships. When he comes back to the court with murder in his heart to find not only his father dead but his sister mad, we will feel for him and see how all that love is turned to poison – 'To cut his throat in the church'; an easy victim for Claudius to manipulate.

The text will always tell you how to play the parts in a human way. Rosencrantz and Guildenstern are boyhood friends. Hamlet is pleased to see them, they to see him. Because they are concerned for him, and flattered by the King, they betray him. But they are not villains, they are genuinely distressed by Hamlet's treatment of them. Horatio is another friend, Ophelia a lover, Polonius a man Hamlet once admired. Play those simple relationships and many of the problems of the play disappear. Above all, think all the time 'Can I recognise these characters in real life?' If the answer is 'no' the fault is certainly yours not Shakespeare's.

I could, of course, go on through the play scene by scene, explaining how we tried to do it, but that would simply give you a rather dead impression of a production which has now joined the hundreds of *Hamlets* of the past centuries. What I would hope is that when students go to the theatre to see Shakespearean productions they go well-armed to challenge that production, both as a creative production, in that it remains essentially true to the playwright's intentions, and as a piece of theatre, in that it has bridged the gap of the centuries and made the play alive now, as opposed to being an exhumed corpse.

Another thing I try to do for actors is to demythologise Shakespeare himself. We tend to think of him as a superman, a cultural giant far beyond our reach, the fitting object for a tourist pilgrimage to Stratford. At my son's school there is an annual outing to Stratford to see Ann Hathaway's Cottage or any exhibition going, but they never see the plays! Shakespeare was a man of the theatre. He was a leading actor, he was a theatre manager and he built two theatres. He wrote for a group of actors whom he knew very well and whom he tried to please. Above all, he wrote to please audiences. He pleased the groundlings as well as the court. He was, dare I say it, a hack. He wrote for the Box Office. His plays are only worth studying as pieces of theatre striving to hold the mirror up to nature, otherwise they lose their purpose.

Actors are also dragged under, as I'm sure students are, by the sheer weight of critical material. My advice to actors is this: 'Arm yourself with C. T. Onions' *A Shakespeare Glossary* and work until you understand the text. When you have understood the text and formed a personal relationship with it, then by all means turn to works of criticism. Approach them with the knowledge that ninety-five per cent will be of no use, because they will be highly subjective academic essays which have nothing to do with the life of the theatre — then you won't be overawed by what you read. The other five per cent will be useful, but, there again, don't be dominated by other peoples' views.'

I don't want to sound as if I am against academics. I hope I have explained that in order to direct Shakespeare responsibly you have first to analyse most rigorously and understand the text. You have to wade through page after page of suggested emendations; you must compare texts and you must find out as much as you can about the play. But all this is done in order to create something dynamic. Anything that doesn't contribute to the life of the play should be ruthlessly jettisoned.

I believe that Teacher and Director have an immense task on their hands. Shakespeare is out of fashion, especially in this audio-visual age. He belongs to the past, he is intellectual culture of the most boring kind, he has nothing to do with the problems of today. This could *not* be further from the truth. I have never read any other writer who knew as much about things as they are now and, indeed, who had such a clear vision of what they might be. It is our duty to unlock the old box and bring out the treasure. It is just as dazzling now as it ever was. The great thing is to treat each play as a live thing. Here the director has a great advantage over the teacher. He is working in the same environment as Shakespeare and trying to achieve the same ends. What I have tried to suggest in this short essay is that the teacher could try to introduce the theatre into his classroom and his classroom to the theatre. The more this is done, the more the student is connected to the play as a vital thing. Willie Fluff knew all about that!

Starting Shakespeare

NEIL KING

To which age group is it best to introduce Shakespeare
for the first time? Many factors will determine a teacher's
(or head of department's) decision. I have always introduced Shakespeare at third-year (13+) level. At this age
pupils' general usage and understanding of language are
blossoming, their insights are beginning to focus on more
complex human affairs, and yet they retain a fair
amount of pre-adolescent enthusiasm, which I hope to
direct towards Shakespeare. During this year I give a
fairly full course on Elizabethan drama, using one
Shakespeare play as a core around which I promote some
investigation into the history, politics, social customs,
music, painting, architecture, attitudes and so forth of
the age. So much the better if I can persuade other
departments in the school to co-operate with me and
synchronise their teaching with my project.

One of my colleagues would like to introduce Shakespeare in the first or second year and I resist this. I have
experimented at 11+ and 12+: Shakespeare's stories can
be simplified and elucidated for these groups, and
teaching can begin here, given the most patient and
imaginative of approaches, but the language is just too
high a hurdle to attempt, and I have found myself
making so many compromises that I can hardly claim to
be dealing with Shakespeare's plays. This is not to deny

that the very young can appreciate Shakespeare. Many years ago some first-year pupils sneaked into the front row of an after-school showing of the Russian film of *Hamlet*, which had been hired for the benefit of the A level candidates. I knew that they intended merely to escape from the cold while they waited for their buses to arrive. Most left after a few minutes; but three or four were seen to beat their breasts, like the ancient mariner's wedding-guest, when the time for their bus came and went – for they could not choose but hear. Of course, they missed more than their bus while watching the film, and misunderstood much, but then so do I whenever I see a Shakespeare play. They stayed, watched, listened and enjoyed *Hamlet* on their own level. If we refrain from embarking on a voyage of discovery until we are quite ready for anything we come across, then everything will remain forever unexplored. Had my wife and I been able to find a baby-sitter we would never have done such a ridiculous thing as to take our three-year-old daughter to a performance of *Cymbeline*; but it was an open-air production on a warm summer's evening, and she would doubtless fall asleep. She did not fall asleep. She enjoyed it. Who should judge the level of her appreciation?

I do not introduce Shakespeare into a void. He makes his entry in the third year (13+) as a part of a continuing history of drama which is, broadly speaking, taught from the first year to the fifth. (This does not mean that all plays or other drama introduced during those years are geared to a chronological approach.) First-year groups discover the Greeks and the Romans in order that they may understand the genesis of western drama. They learn something of the worship of Dionysus; of Thespis, Aeschylus, Sophocles, Euripedes, Aristophanes, Plautus and Terence; of Athenian festivals, theatres and amphitheatres, masks, costumes, choruses and audiences; and, most importantly, of the traditional language of the theatre, for it is a great advantage if pupils arrive at Shakespeare having absorbed, at a simplified level, such notions as 'tragedy' and 'comedy'. For much of this teaching I use my own *Classical Beginnings*, which is the first book in the Hulton Drama Series: the introduction, illustrations and 'Things to do' sections are a conflation of my own notes and materials, gathered and used over the years, together with modernised edited versions of Euripedes' *Bacchae*, Aristophanes' *Clouds* and Plautus's *The Swaggering Soldier*. I never use with any one group all the material contained in the book, but a common core of essential matter is always covered. Another useful book is Kenneth McLeish's *Four Greek Plays* (Longman) which contains an entertaining *Archarnians* and a powerful *Oedipus*. Interdisciplinary co-operation on an *ad hoc* basis is always fun, and it is a good idea to try to persuade the art and craft department to get the first years designing a painted backcloth for a Greek play or a street scene for a Roman play, or making theatrical masks.

During the second year, an attempt is made to cover the period of almost two millennia which separates the ancient world from that of Shakespeare. Between the plays of Plautus and Terence and the very first plays of mediaeval Europe there stretches a gap of a thousand years. During the final years of the Roman Empire no great plays were written, and those already in existence were read rather than acted. It seems, at first sight, that there is a complete break between the classical tradition and the rise of mediaeval Church drama and Mystery plays. However, the dramatic spirit was kept alive by the kind of entertainers who would still have been around in Shakespeare's day – jugglers, acrobats, fire-eaters, stilt-walkers, animal-trainers with monkeys and bears, mummers and mime artists and, most important of all, by ballad-singers and story-tellers. It is probable that, even in the Dark Ages, the wandering minstrel with his songs and stories of heroes, such as Beowulf, brought entertainment to those huddled round some hearth.

I explain that the new dramatic tradition began, in fact, with none of these performers. It grew up in the churches. We do not know all the reasons for this, but we can see that drama grew out of an extension of religious ceremony and ritual in a way that helped to make religious themes more vivid and easily understood by ordinary folk. I go on to show how the three main

59

ingredients of drama which Shakespeare unconsciously uses in everything he wrote for the stage – namely, impersonation (characterisation), dialogue and action – grew out of the requirements of staging in a church. The way in which drama emerged in the mediaeval church and then outgrew it is a valuable lesson in how the instinct to dramatise is irrepressible, and how plays will adapt themselves to the acting space available. This will help pupils the following year to understand how much of the stagecraft of Shakespeare's plays is directly attributable to the dimensions of the sixteenth-century inn-yard and bear-baiting pit. After illustrating church drama, I explain the process by which the maturing drama escaped the confines of ecclesiastical buildings and developed into a secular activity. The course centres upon a consideration of Mystery plays in the market-place. Sometimes, with a good class, I look at Morality plays (an understanding of 'the Vice in the old play' helps when we come to Falstaff). I mention mumming plays and other folk traditions, such as the Padstow Hobby-horse. Then we consider the emergence of itin-erant acting troupes, regarded as little better than rogues and vagabonds, who began to travel the roads a century before Shakespeare, putting on plays and enter-tainments at fairs, in inn-yards, and in the great halls of rich men's houses (mention *Hamlet* and *The Taming of the Shrew*, and use C. Walter Hodges' drawings – see bibliography). A particularly interesting link with Elizabethan drama is an episode in the anonymous play *Sir Thomas More*, scenes in which may have been written by Shakespeare. More lived in a splendid house in Chelsea, and, in the extract below, a troupe such as would have been on the road in Shakespeare's time have called at the house. The reference to the Lord Cardinal's Players shows that great men were beginning to patronise companies of actors, subsidising them financi-ally and expecting them to perform on important occasions.

More.   Welcome, good friend; what is your will with
           me?

Player. My lord, my fellows and myself
　　　　Are come to tender you our willing service,
　　　　So please you to command us.
More. What for a play, you mean?
　　　　Whom do ye serve?
Player. My Lord Cardinal's grace.
More. My Lord Cardinal's Players! Now, trust me,
　　　　welcome!
　　　　You happen hither in lucky time.
　　　　To pleasure me, and benefit yourselves.
　　　　The Mayor of London and some Aldermen,
　　　　His lady and their wives, are my kind guests
　　　　This night at supper. Now, to have a play
　　　　Before the banquet will be excellent.
　　　　I prithee, tell me, what plays have ye?

The player runs through his repertoire until he mentions
a play called *The Marriage of Wit and Wisdom*, where-
upon Sir Thomas More cries, 'That, my lads, I'll none
but that! The theme is very good.' He turns quickly to a
servant who is standing nearby and says:

　　　　Go, make him drink, and all his fellows too.
　　　　How many are ye?
Player. Four men and a boy.
More. But one boy? Then I see,
　　　　There's but few women in the play.
Player. Three, my lord; Dame Science, Lady Vanity,
　　　　And Wisdom – she herself.
More. And one boy to play them all? By'r Lady, he's
　　　　loaden!
　　　　Well, my good fellows, get ye straight together,
　　　　And make ye ready with what haste ye may.

But the performance is delayed while one of the players
runs to the next village to fetch a beard for young Wit.
More immediately steps into the breach and plays the
part of Wit himself. After the play the actors are paid
and given supper and lodging for the night.
　　Groups of travelling players still exist, and in recent
years I have been fortunate that the Medieval Players,

a troupe based at 192, Goswell Road, London, have come once or twice a year to perform in Hull, and I have been able to make a visit to see them the climax of the course.

In teaching this course I use my own book *Mystery and Morality* (Hulton Drama Series). Apart from the necessary background material it contains edited and adapted texts of *Noah's Flood, The Coventry Nativity Play, Everyman* and *Ralph Roister Doister.*

And so to the third year, and Shakespeare. Where is it best to start? Is it better to begin with the text of a play and then move outwards into 'background' material? Or should the Elizabethan world be presented first? The answer depends upon your central reason for studying Shakespeare. I consider that the text is central and that a consideration of the culture in which Shakespeare lived should grow from a study of his plays, not vice-versa. I commence by casting parts for a reading of the first scene of my chosen play, and as we proceed I begin to place Shakespeare in the context of a bustling Renaissance city of some 200,000 inhabitants where there was much music, fighting, laughter and skulduggery, and where many other good playwrights rivalled Shakespeare for trade drawn from a population where theatre-going was as popular as football is today. With hindsight, we may see Shakespeare and his players as the only team in the first division, but the audiences of the time did not see things in that light. I draw in a consideration of the playhouses, showing how they grew out of a combination of the innyard and the bear-baiting pit and how they often dictate the stagecraft of our play. I use material from the introductions of my own *Elizabethan Comedy* and *Elizabethan Tragedy* (Hulton Drama Series) and other sources (see below and the bibliography at the end of this essay).

Which is the best play to choose? I hate anthologies. I want to introduce pupils to the shape of a whole play and to the feel of a complete dramatic plot. Until recently I have selected from a collection entitled *Presenting Shakespeare* (Harrap), edited by R. C. Peat. This contains reduced versions of *A Midsummer Night's Dream, Macbeth, The Merchant of Venice* and *Twelfth Night.*

Peat has reproduced the best scenes from the plays, linking them with narrative from Charles and Mary Lamb's *Tales from Shakespeare.* A battered set of Peat has carried me through many years but the Lamb prose, while splendid in itself, is not suited to the task for which Peat has press-ganged it; and the retained scenes are uncut, thus keeping difficult passages and lines from which the pupil could be saved. I have begun to compile my own edited editions of Shakespeare, using the same basic method as Peat, but writing my own narrative bridges and cutting down scenes which I have retained in a way designed to make fluent and digestible what is left. I do not regard this as bowdlerising. I am doing the same as a theatre director who works for a modern audience: Adrian Noble rightly cut nearly 600 lines of *Henry V* for his 1984 production at Stratford. I do the same for my audience (who are, of course, the actors too!). I never rewrite à la Rowse, apart from the occasional word here or there (for instance, it seems reasonable to change 'kennel' to 'gutter' in *The Taming of the Shrew*; not even the rhythm of the line is affected). Where I have cut the text I try to maintain the pattern of blank verse lines.[1]

Below is a summary of my feelings about the plays commonly thought appropriate for younger Shakespeareans, followed by detailed notes on how I might work my way through *Henry IV, part 1.* The ability and sex of a class, together with a teacher's personal enthusiasms, will affect choice.

Twelfth Night This play has good variety. Much can be explored by considering the degree of sympathy which each character evokes in an audience. Malvolio presents an interesting study for a psychiatrist's case-book. At appropriate points in a study of the play I have shown posters and pictures of great Elizabethan ladies (Olivia), powerful lords (Orsino), gallants (Sebastian, Sir Andrew Aguecheek), courtiers (Valentine, Curio) and tavern revellers at the Mermaid (Sir Toby Belch). I never miss the opportunity during Act II Scene 3 to gather together some singers and perform the catch 'Hold Thy Peace' as a round-song.² It is not necessary to select those in the class who can sing well; indeed, a random collection of four volunteers will make the more appropriate the climax when Maria rushes in hissing 'What a cater-wauling do you keep here!' The box-tree episode in Act II Scene 5 provides more 'theatrical' fun: Sir Toby, Sir Andrew and Fabian can hide under/behind/on top of/ inside whatever a classroom has to offer; and in summertime it is worth taking the class outside to the nearest available shrubbery.

The Taming of the Shrew Often considered to be a nasty piece, this play goes well if edited and presented in an appropriate way. There is much stimulus for a discussion of the battle of the sexes, and the basic situation can even be placed, with a good class, within the context of the debate over the place of women in marriage. I suspect that this will need careful handling in schools with an Asian community. The image of Petruchio taming Kate as a falconer does a hawk will be a real one to a class which has read *Kes*. An advantage of using this play in the third or fourth year is that it is rarely set at 16+ level. It is good if a teacher has access to the BBC production with John Cleese as Petruchio; this is one of the best of this predominantly dreary series.

Romeo and Juliet This appears to be an obvious choice, but I tend to avoid it at this level. As well as the love theme, the play is full of a violence and hatred with which I do not particularly want to deal with thirteen-year-olds. All teachers will find that there are texts which are the backbone of others' teaching at a particular level but which they themselves would leave alone. One colleague says: 'If the group contains girls, I often opt for *Romeo and Juliet*'. He has a view of the central preoccupations of the play which allows him to work on it in a particular way. The Zeffirelli film is very useful.

A Midsummer Night's Dream Careful decisions must be taken as to which parts of this play are to be dwelt

upon and which cut. I have had great fun with this play.
I have used it to demonstrate how Shakespeare may
have cast the nineteen or so members of the Chamber-
lain's Men to best effect. (The company clown – Will
Kemp? – for Bottom, Burbage doubling as Theseus/
Oberon, the best boy actor as Hippolyta/Titania.) Wher-
ever possible, I make points which are clear on stage,
but which are not obvious when the play is read. It is
necessary to convey the nature of the fairies at an early
stage. I was very lucky in 1983 when I managed to take
a group to see the Royal Shakespeare touring production
directed by Sheila Hancock. One of many results was
the change of epithets used to describe the fairies: 'silly',
'wet', 'poofter', and so forth gave way to 'frightening',
'supernatural', 'grotesque' and even 'mortal-baiting'. I
have had much fun with the play-within-the-play.

The mechanicals are not central to the play, but they
are there, and can be used to good effect when teaching
at this level. To stage the play-within-the-play on its
own is no new thing, and, although world-weary Shakespeareans may find it tiresome, the young do not. I divide
the class into five groups, each taking one of the parts
of Bottom, Quince, Starveling, Snout, Snug and Flute.
Sometimes I select six producers (Quince), and allow
them to choose their teams, picking in turn and bearing
in mind the castings that they need. Groups are then
each given a scene to work on. After eventual performance, usually with books in hands (although some are
keen to do more than merely 'look o'er their parts'), the
best group or two are selected by the class. There is some
swapping of parts – if necessary – under my guidance,
and the final versions are performed in front of the rest of
the class. Sometimes the best one is put on as lunchtime
drama, when anyone in the school who wishes can come
to watch. Over the years I have done this with three
groups, and each time the motley audience which has
wandered in, perhaps simply to get out of the cold, has
thoroughly enjoyed itself. It surprises me how often
professional productions manage to make the rude mechanicals stuffy and boring. Perhaps the young understand

something about the essence of their comedy which adults have forgotten.

Henry V This is a much more interesting and less straightforward play than is often thought. If possible, I like to 'team-teach' Henry the man in association with the form's history teacher. He or she presents the historical person, I present Shakespeare's; pupils are soon able to point, without prompting, at elements in Shakespeare's portrait which show that he is not simply presenting Henry as hero-warrior-king, nor is he intending that the audience adopt a naïvely patriotic stance. The Chorus excellently demonstrates why the language is important, and how Shakespeare had to use poetry to paint the scenery and light the setting of a cold night or rainy day at Agincourt. He only had words with which to transport his audience away from the reality of three o'clock in the afternoon of a late spring day in London, 1600:

> Now entertain conjecture of a time
> When creeping murmur and the poring dark
> Fills the wide vessel of the universe.
> From camp to camp, through the foul womb of
>   night,
> The hum of either army stilly sounds,
> That the fix'd sentinels almost receive
> The secret whispers of each other's watch.
> Fire answers fire, and through their paly flames
> Each battle sees the other's umber'd face;
> Steed threatens steed, in high and boastful
>   neighs
> Piercing the night's dull ear; and from the tents
> The armourers accomplishing the knights,
> With busy hammers closing rivets up,
> Give dreadful note of preparation.
> The country cocks do crow, the clocks do toll,
> And the third hour of drowsy morning name.

It is well worth investing in a video copy of the 1944 Laurence Olivier film of *Henry V* (available through

Rank Video, P. O. Box 70, Great West Road, Brentford, Middlesex TW8 9HR). The first twenty minutes of the film can be bought on its own, and this is worth obtaining regardless of which play you decide to study. The opening scenes are staged in a recreation of The Globe and, although recent research has modified previous notions of Elizabethan performance circumstances, Olivier's version is more than good enough for teaching and for the generation of enthusiasm on first looking into Shakespeare. It is particularly useful if your video-player has freeze-frame facilities: pupils can make notes and sketches while the picture is held.

Macbeth This play has everything, and the individual teacher can choose from a variety of ways of approaching it. One wrong way is to use the play as the merest springboard for a thematic study of evil: it is surprising how often this sin is committed. One of my colleagues, who engages in as much scenic effect as possible when reading a Shakespeare play in class, has been known to bring in a forest of potted plants from his home in order to create a moving Birnam Wood – a great deal of fuss, of course, but his pupils will always remember that scene. On a recent course, I met a drama teacher who was vehement in his denunciation of those who touched this play before 'A' level: he strongly felt that pupils would misunderstand much and completely miss more. I have already mentioned my reaction to this attitude. I always tell my pupils studying *Macbeth* or any other play at this level that they should not worry too much if they suspect that they are missing things, but that they should work away at their awareness and half-awareness and should ask about these areas, developing therefrom their understanding of the play.

Much Ado About Nothing This is not a play which I had thought of using in class until I directed a stage production of it; the wit of Beatrice and Benedick seemed to be 'A' level material. Yet, after I had extensively cut the play, I realised that many themes can be made accessible at more junior levels, where ideas of discontented, illegitimate, younger brothers, the superficiality of 'clever' people, the danger of judging by appearances, the irony of incompetent people solving the crime – all these and more could be understood. Dogberry and the Watch is great fun, of course. So I tried out my cut version on a group of third-year boys and it worked quite well. I suspect that it may go better with a mixed or all-girl class, and that it must be avoided with a poor class of any complexion.

Love's Labour's Lost This needs to be heavily cut, of course; but think of the marvellous story! Look with the pupils at various historical attempts to set up exclusive sects, groups, communes, and then work through selected scenes. Parts of this play go down surprisingly well. The attempt of the village schoolmaster, teacher, constable and swain together with the swaggering soldier to put on a pageant for royalty is wonderful workshop material. Back in 1972 I successfully used this extract with thirteen-year-olds in a school Elizabethan Evening.

Hamlet Exclusively 'A' level material? Not a bit of it – and I have argued this theme with a hostile English adviser. At a superficial level there are murders, spies, pirates, comic gravediggers, a ghost and a duel and much more; and on a more profound level a thirteen-year-old can cope with the dilemma of a modern, sensitive, thinking man who is given a primitive command to 'Revenge!' and who learns that violence, however apparently justified, is corrupting. Tell them about the Anglo-Saxon notion of *wergeld* (compensation paid to a murdered man's family to prevent revenge-killing and end blood-feud); look at moments in their own lives where pupils have wanted revenge (what did it achieve?); quote snippets of Francis Bacon's essay *Of Revenge*; trace the four revengers in the play (Fortinbras, Hamlet, Pyrrhus, Laertes) and examine their different motives for seeking revenge; illustrate how many old Western films and modern T.V. 'cops' series use the revenge motive as a trigger for the plot. It is not too difficult for pupils to see how the audience can sympathise with

Hamlet's desire for vengeance while recognising that personal revenge is morally and legally unacceptable in the world outside the theatre.

Henry IV, part 1 If I had to choose one play for thirteen-year-olds, this would be it: it may not plumb the profundities or rise to the great heights of some of Shakespeare's plays, but there is history, comedy, politics, fantasy – even a touch of romance. The characters are varied and memorable especially, of course, that 'fat paunch' Falstaff. The following notes are a conflation of various approaches I have used.

I 1 At the beginning of the play the politics must be made accessible. Sketch the scenario of a weary boss who is beset by problems. Cast parts and read the scene. Invite questions on difficult words. Look at metaphors. Consider the father who, with all the burdens of running a country, has an irresponsible son and heir who hits town whenever possible. Would Henry be a chain-smoker in a modern dress production? At what time of the day or night would you set this scene if you were to direct a modern dress production? Two in the morning? What is there in the text that gives this feel to the scene? Give some historical background to the scene (will their history teacher do this?). Put on blackboard a simplified royal family tree. Any more modern analogies to be drawn? Pupils to draw an outline map of the country and mark on it any places mentioned in this and any other scene in the play. Find and mark the power bases of the nobility mentioned in the play. (Will their geography teacher co-operate here and elsewhere? If not, issue worksheets.)

I 2 Pub scene. Post-binge hangover? Introduction to Falstaff and Prince Hal. Implications of Prince's soliloquy at the end of scene – a calculating character? Not really one of the lads? Just slumming?

I 3 Council chamber. Serious politics. Rebellion. Is direct action against authority ever justified? Tell them what Henry (as Bolingbroke) did to Richard II. Dwell on Hotspur's image of the 'popinjay' (why would this court fop have got right up Hotspur's nose?). Show pictures of

Elizabethan gentlemen and dandies. (Opportunities for Art Department to help here and elsewhere. Illustrations to the play? Design settings?)

II 1 Draw on blackboard and/or give out photocopies of sketches illustrating Elizabethan innyard. Demonstrate its suitability for performance of plays (if not already done). Imagine early in the morning, sleepy ostlers unable to stir themselves, carriers (equivalent to long-distance lorry drivers) getting ready to move on. Gadshill (what's a 'setter'?) arouses suspicions as he tries to find out information in order to set up the robbery.

II 2 Robbery on Gadshill — the place! Introduce a little action here if pupils have so far kept to their desks. Make a clearing, non-actors stay seated and be trees, cameras roll!

II 3 Difficult at this age. Not very dramatic. Girls may have some insight into Kate's position, boys have none. Scene could be cut – a case for a narrative bridge.

II 4 Another pub scene. Read until entry of Falstaff (or cut Francis business) then break for introduction to taverns and stews of the South Bank. Do not be squeamish about the brothel trade: the pupils can take it. Sketch map on board and/or issue outline of sixteenth–century London, making them fill in details now and as the play proceeds. Make clear that audiences would have passed many taverns and brothels as they went through red light district on their way to the play-house via ferry or London Bridge. This scene in play is going on in real life not fifty yards from the Globe itself. Get Falstaff enthroned on a desk for the 'play extempore'. This episode never fails. One of my colleagues was engaged on this, an *Adidas* bag crowning an elevated Falstaff, who was waving a pencil case (sceptre) and bawling over the heads of the class's wild hilarity when word came that the Headmaster (sheriff?) and one or two other teachers (monstrous watch?) were at the door seeking to restore order over the Lord of Misrule (my colleague?). After this scene has been studied spend time on the Falstaff phenomenon. Show how the braggart soldier, who is full of bluster but is actually a coward, has always been a popular figure on the stage. Dip into

Plautus's *The Swaggering Soldier* (in *Classical Beginnings*, pp 67–95) and *Ralph Roister Doister* (*Mystery and Morality* pp 61–96). Look ahead to Pistol. The films/videos of *Chimes at Midnight* and *Henry V* are available, but perhaps best kept for later. Show some (more?) of Walter Hodges's pictures.

III 1 Elements of Glendower's character are fun, but there's not much else in this scene for thirteen-year-olds. Cut entire and replace by narrative bridge.

III 2 Father-son interview ending in good measure of reconciliation. Not all that exciting on the page, but pupils must cope with it. Use notion of generation gap: son wanting to do things differently. Illustrate change of tone at end of scene: Blunt thrusts warfare to the forefront. The time of politics, taverns, robberies, etc., must be suspended. More places to write on to the map.

III 3 Pub. How Falstaff and the low-life characters will be affected by the war. This scene needs some cutting.

IV 1 The Rebel camp. Help to generate feeling of bustle and activity as this scene is read. Some editing needed. Use Hotspur's behaviour in this scene to move towards a more traditional consideration of character, something which is important in literary studies (and not merely in examinations).

IV 2 Falstaff's private army. A good opportunity to push back the desks and act out the scene. Minimal props needed, and a cleared classroom is as good a set as any.

IV 3 Rebel camp. Percy's. A little about the conventions of mediaeval warfare. This scene needs cutting. Could be omitted and narrative bridge used.

IV 4 Cut.

V 1 Day of the battle. Show how words are used to paint the scene in the opening six lines so that the imagination of the audience is stimulated. Play audiotape of the opening of any scene in a radio play: show how the sounds of hospital, railway station, nineteenth-century room or whatever are established and then 'faded down'. Shakespeare is doing the same. Dwell on Falstaff's commentary on honour. Discuss it. Modern notion of honourable behaviour?

V 2   Can be cut, except for Hotspur's speech at the end of the scene rallying his troops for battle.

V 3   The battle. Single combat. Perhaps a look at armour and fighting conditions. Sir Walter Blunt's honour?

V 4   A one-lesson scene. Read it, then go to audio-visual room and watch battle footage from Orson Welles' *Chimes at Midnight*. If time, or next lesson, contrast with more romantic view in Olivier's film of *Henry V*.

V 5   Conclusion. Note the Prince's act of courtesy towards Douglas and discuss chivalry. Note how ending of play sets up a sequel.

In addition to the opportunities suggested in this synopsis, there are many other things to do along the way. Pupils could:

– see other scenes from *Chimes at Midnight*.

– Design a set for *Henry IV, part 1* suitable for staging a production in the school hall/theatre, especially bearing in mind (1) Elizabethan performance conditions (2) the advantages and weaknesses of the performance area (3) how modern lighting can be used to effect.

– Hear recordings of appropriate Elizabethan music as background. Choose music appropriate to certain moments and moods in the play. (Could the music department be brought in here?)

– Write a biography/autobiography of William Shakespeare, Richard Burbage or any other theatrical notable they have discovered during the course.

– Write a dialogue in which a theatre 'fan' of the 1590s argues with a Puritan over the benefits/social corruption resulting from the performance of plays.

– Construct a model of The Globe. Kits are available, especially in Stratford-upon-Avon.

– Visit Stratford-upon-Avon for a performance by the RSC and related tours, visits and so forth.

– Imagine that they are part of an eager crowd crossing London Bridge or catching the river ferry in order to see the first performance of *Henry IV, part 1* at a public Elizabethan theatre (no matter that this probably occurred at the Theatre in Finsbury fields). After the performance they write in their diaries a detailed account of the day, and their description has become a famous source of knowledge about the Elizabethan theatre. They should include as much detail as they can about *all* aspects of the theatre.

– Having heard the story of the players arriving at Sir Thomas More's house, write it from the point of view of one of the players who recalls the occasion after hearing of More's execution.

– During time of plague the theatres were closed. Small groups of actors went on tour. Imagine them arriving at a great house to perform extracts of *Henry IV, part 1* (*The Taming of the Shrew* lends itself to this exercise).

– Write a piece of dramatic script in which a company of Elizabethan actors discuss the casting and production of *Henry IV, part 1*. Perhaps Shakespeare himself is present, which could make criticism of the play rather embarrassing!

–Arrange an evening of Elizabethan entertainment, including dancing, music, skittles, bowls, puppets (which were popular at fairs), wrestling, conjuring, a masque and extracts from *Henry IV, part 1* (Other extracts which work well are Bottom's play from Act V of *A Midsummer Night's Dream*; the Pageant of the Nine Worthies from Act V of *Love's Labour's Lost*; and the scenes of Jack Cade's rebellion from *Henry VI, part 2*. A highpoint of the evening could be a visit by Queen Elizabeth and her courtiers to watch the entertainment.

– Arrange a full-scale production of *Henry IV, part 1,* trying to involve musicians, artists, wood-workers and other departments in the school.

– As opportunities arise from the text, be introduced to study matter dealing with the actors, audience, dramatic techniques, stagecraft, rival companies and other circumstances surrounding Elizabethan theatre (see the introductions to *Elizabethan Comedy* and *Elizabethan Tragedy* in the Hulton Drama Series).

– Visit the Bear Gardens Museum which stands on the site of the old bear-baiting pit in Southwark, London.

– Invent a card game or board game based on the plot and characters of a Shakespeare play. All hazard cards must utilise quotations from the play.

– Initiate a project for the whole class which aims to re-create a busy London day in, say, 1597 (see how Keith Dewhurst has done this for an Oxfordshire village of the 1880s in *Lark Rise* [Hutchinson], his dramatic adaptation of part of Flora Thompson's book *Lark Rise to Candleford*). All the previously mentioned departments in the school can be drawn in, and economic advisers will be needed to boot.

BIBLIOGRAPHY

From the enormous industry which lives and feeds upon the body of Shakespeare's plays, the following is a short list of books which I have found useful in the teaching of Shakespeare to younger pupils (and to older ones).

Eric Boagey *Starting Shakespeare*, University Tutorial Press, Slough, 1983.

Boagey's approach is lively, including mock interviews with luminaries of the Elizabethan theatre, production notes, annotated scenes (from the production, as opposed to the literary, viewpoint), checkpoint (that is, revision) questions, comprehension questions, lots of pictures and imaginative snippets. All excellent stuff if it fires pupils. However, too often the froth has been creamed off Shakespeare's text and splashed about the book, which gives the impression that the text as a whole is rather a bore. The drawback of this jazzed-up, 'relevant' approach is that enthusiastic and imaginative teachers will not find much that is new in the book, and unimaginative teachers will not be led to see how good things can be naturally drawn out of the text.

Jim Bradbury *Shakespeare and His Theatre*, Then and There series, Longman, London, 1975.

A thorough little book which, as you might expect from the title, combines a biography of Shakespeare with a survey of the theatre in which he worked. Liberally illustrated with black-and-white photographs, prints and diagrams. At £1.25 it is worth considering the purchase of a few of these.

John Russell Brown *Shakespeare and His Theatre*, Kestrel (Penguin), Harmondsworth, 1983.

An expensive but beautiful book. The text is clear, concise and easy to read, giving just the right amount of information. David Gentleman's illustrations are light and bright without being fanciful or frivolous. A delightful book to hold, but not to be put into hands which have come unwashed from the games field.

Anthony Burgess *Shakespeare*, Jonathan Cape, London, 1970.

Reprinted Penguin, Harmondsworth, 1972.

A good coffee-table book. The text is beyond junior pupils, but there are plenty of good illustrations. A bright 'O' level pupil who is thinking of pursuing an English course in the sixth form will find the book a good stimulus.

C. Walter Hodges *Shakespeare and the Players*, Bell, London, 1973.

Patronising in places, but on the whole a pleasant and easy-to-read little book which gives an outline of what we know or may reasonably suppose of Shakespeare's involvement with actors from boyhood until retirement in Stratford. Delightful pen and ink drawings by Walter Hodges himself include illustrations of strolling players, London, playhouses and so forth, and there is a chapter which gives an imaginary account of a performance of *Richard III* in the Globe.

C. Walter Hodges *Shakespeare's Theatre*, Oxford University Press, 1964.

An excellent introduction to mediaeval drama leads to an excellent tour through Shakespeare's theatre. Again, both text and illustrations (colour) are by Walter Hodges, and the book exudes the lively enthusiasm which he feels for his· theme. I use this book extensively in my teaching. If I had to choose one from this bibliography to take to my desert island, this would be it.

Neil King *Elizabethan Comedy*, Hulton Drama Series, Amersham, 1984.

Illustrated introduction to Elizabethan theatre plus cut versions of *The Shoemaker's Holiday, Volpone* and *The Knight of the Burning Pestle*.

Neil King *Elizabethan Tragedy*, Hulton Drama Series, Amersham, 1984.
Illustrated introduction to Elizabethan theatre plus cut versions of *Doctor Faustus, The Duchess of Malfi* and *The Witch of Edmonton.*
Robert Leach *The Elizabethan Theatre*, Harrap Theatre Workshop Series, London, 1978.
The laudable aim of the author is that the theatre of the period should be related to other studies, such as history, geography, music, art, craft and so on. There are many companion volumes in this series and many opportunities presented, but teachers must think about their objectives before using sections.

Finally, I have two battered sets of Jackdaws (Jonathan Cape resource folders): No. 9 (*Young Shakespeare*) and No. 54 (*Shakespeare's Theatre*), and have found them very useful over the years; but they are currently out of print. It is worth putting pressure on Cape to reprint.

NOTES
1 Copies of my editions can be obtained by writing to me at 1 Woodlands, Beverley, East Yorkshire HU17 8BT.
2 The full catch – not given in the text of *Twelfth Night* – runs:
    Hold thy peace
    And I prithee hold thy peace
    Thou knave
    Hold thy peace
There is, of course, an obscene quibble (or two) on 'peace'. The musical notation is as follows:

Approaches to Shakespeare at A level

PETER HOLLINDALE

Principles and Practice

Members of my family who are experienced drivers have strong views about the statutory driving test. 'First of all you pass the test,' they say, 'and then you learn to drive.' The driving test, they feel, proves only that you know and can apply certain fixed rules of the road. Although these may be important, they are only a first stage towards the art, skill and enjoyment of driving, and in the first stages of driving instruction the imperative need to pass the test takes precedence over genuine driving experience. That comes with practice, later, when the mind is not so obsessively targeted on passing an exam.

The analogy with sixth–form Shakespeare work is a daunting one for teachers. In A level work, too, there is an exam to be passed. In A level work, too, there is a question of art, skill and enjoyment. Just as in learning to drive, the learning process that best fits the first objective may not be in the interests of the second. Why not, then, accept the examination imperative for what it is and leave the art, skill and enjoyment for later? Unfortunately there is a crucial difference. You take the driving test because you want to be able to drive – the motivation and the subsequent experience can be taken for granted.

No one takes the driving test merely to acquire a bit of paper saying he has passed it. Alas, that is *precisely* what many A level students 'doing' Shakespeare have in mind. They want, and need, a bit of paper which says they have 'passed' English Literature at A level. Once they have got it, there is no particular reason why they should ever look at Shakespeare or any other major author again, unless they want to.

Any sixth form English teacher worth entrusting with the task will feel that if the two-year A level course produces such an outcome it has been almost wholly futile, a waste of time, and perhaps even worse than not having done the course at all. For the candidate there may be incidental advantages, of a kind which differ from the driving test analogy. If you pass your driving test, no one is going to believe that this constitutes an intrinsic qualification for you to become a teacher or a steeplejack (though it may be a useful ancillary aid, enabling you to get to the school or the steeple). If, on the other hand, you pass A level English Literature with a respectable grade, gullible persons in higher education may decide that this makes all the difference between you and a sixth form rival if you both want to study for a degree in Economics or Law. This is, of course, nonsense, but, since it is deep set, institutionalised nonsense, the teacher is compelled to take account of it. He may well envy the driving instructor his highly-motivated, single-minded student, who is learning to drive in order to drive.

For the teacher of Shakespeare, then, there can or should be no question of teaching for the test and letting the art come later. Somehow, the A level course has to deal effectively with both.

The first thing the Shakespeare teacher must do, then, is to ask a question and be prepared to give it a difficult, principled answer. The question is, 'What is the purpose of studying Shakespeare at A level?' A part of the answer is 'to pass an examination at the end of it'. An even better, though thornier, answer is 'to pass an examination with a grade which reflects as accurately as possible the candidate's work and ability rather than the teacher's.' But the examination, if it becomes the *sole* objective and not just an important one, is utilitarian, demoralising and counter-productive even if convenient. The rest of the teacher's answer must relate to the educational experience itself rather than the examination which tests it. So there must be other answers to the question, and I would propose the following in roughly descending order of priority:

i) to arouse or extend the students' interest in a great and widely-performed dramatist, to the extent that for the rest of their lives they will find pleasure and satisfaction in seeing Shakespearean productions and will positively wish to go to them.

ii) to develop competence and confidence in reading a Shakespeare text, and a justified belief that the unavoidable early language barriers are merely a temporary obstacle, can be broken, and are worth breaking, so that reading Shakespeare becomes a dependable – even if irregular and incidental – source of life-long recreation.

iii) to stimulate intelligent pleasure in exploring human character, relationships and predicaments, and awareness that dramatic presentation is a direct and illuminating way of encountering them.

iv) to sharpen realisation that human life is – as it has been aptly called – 'a field of choices', that morality is not an abstract system but the currency of behaviour, and that moral activity is determined by individual character and circumstances. It follows that great drama such as Shakespeare's, which entails a continual blending of moral choice, individual character and heightened particular circumstances, is not locked into an obsolete culture or a distant epoch but maps out a field of choices which is ours as much as his. It is in this sense that Shakespeare is truly 'our contemporary', and that studying his plays is 'relevant' to our own lives.

v) to demonstrate the significance of language, showing that speech *is* significant action, not just a clue to it, and that we can understand people, their behaviour and their relationships much better if we look very closely at the language they use. Shakespeare takes us deeply into that kind of understanding because he enacts human behaviour through language of an unusually concentrated and developed kind. (Therefore, if he is difficult it is usually because he needs to be difficult in order to be exact, not because he is being perverse and inconsiderate or because he is old-fashioned.)

vi) to develop insight into what is commonly called 'the human condition', by which I mean the unavoidable and often painful contingencies of life which lie outside human control. They include the facts of injustice, chance and accident, disaster and death, the tension between the natural and the supernatural, the great metaphysical uncertainties. These are the great questions which it seems unrealistic to expect most sixteen and seventeen year olds to understand, the questions which require philosophical and theological exegesis and have not as yet been laid to rest by it. In drama they generate the equivalent of philosophical concepts in such terms as 'tragedy' and 'comedy', and through their dramatic enactment they are made as human and immediate as they can be anywhere outside the violence of direct personal experience. It is easy to underestimate the ability of teenagers to understand such concepts and the experiences they embody. A useful corrective to under-estimation is to remember that teenagers can and often do confront the reality itself, in their own lives, and cope. The greatness of drama, and Shakespearean greatness above all, is that it is human and actual, flesh and blood. If, as teachers, we define our basic terms carefully and otherwise avoid abstraction, students will repeatedly surprise us by their responsiveness.

vii) to enable insight into what I would term the 'deep structure' of Shakespearean drama. This is a very advanced stage which may be beyond the compass of most A level students. 'Surface structure' is quite a simple matter which is part of 'dramatic presentation' as I referred to it in iii) above. It involves appreciating why a particular speech or scene is effectively (or ineffectively) placed where it is. Most of Shakespeare's opening scenes provide good examples, setting up perspectives, viewpoints, and hints which have immediate impact and guide audience response to what will follow. 'Deep structure' entails a minute attentiveness to the fusion of language, character, incident and theme at single moments which not only have resonances throughout the play as a flow of events but also distil the totality of its imaginative design. Cordelia's 'Nothing, my lord' is a straightforward example: to understand the structural importance of this line is to gather up not only the movement of *King Lear*, as if it were a film, but also its shape, as if it were a photograph. This requires an altogether different level of imaginative penetration, and, although it may rarely be possible to reach it at A level, the possibility should not be overlooked.

This is a sequence of objectives which have to do with diverse and cumulative understanding, integral not to the examination but to the teaching rationale of studying Shakespeare in the first place. The first two relate specifically to Shakespeare. The others could be taught through the agency of other dramatists, though most teachers would still feel that Shakespeare is their supreme exemplar. But first things must be placed first: if teaching Shakespeare is not about *enjoying* Shakespeare, then *all* its other vindications, whether utilitarian or educative, are undermined.

To return to the first question, 'What is the purpose of studying Shakespeare at A level?': the teacher's potential answers are not yet complete. So far we have accounted for the utilitarian (passing the exam), the recreational (enjoying Shakespeare in performance and text) and the dramatically educative (the approach through drama to – progressively – psychological, moral, linguistic, philosophical and aesthetic insights). Running alongside these, and not competing with them for placement in a rank order, are the personal and social skills and confidence which ought to grow from doing A level Shakespeare through an appropriate diversity of activities.

These activities are broadly of three kinds. The first is 'discussion', a term which should be defined generously to include a range of enterprises in articulating response through speech, not just active participation in teacher-led talk. The second is enactment – the approach to drama *through* drama, which may involve improvisation of equivalent contemporary situations or of 'missing' scenes, or exploratory acting of a speech or a scene, comparing interpretations not only through textual commentary but under the test of voice and movement. Enactment may even involve public performance, though this is likely to be less profitable. A serious teaching error is to see enactment as an all-or-nothing choice between full scale production and neglect, when it is the informal intermediate stages which are most likely to deepen understanding. The third activity is writing, and here again an eclectic approach is needed which does not restrict activity to short critical essays or 'answers to old questions'.

I do not regard any of these three activities as dispensable, or even as subject to necessary economies. They all need to be clearly conceived as having a double role. The first role is specifically related to studying Shakespeare, in that each will help the students to *discover*, *define*, *articulate* and *test* their responses to the play. The second involves the development of speech and writing skills which have value in their own right. In the process they should enlarge the personal qualities of confidence, independence, and co-operative enterprise, since the outcome (of written work, properly used, no less than discussion and enactment) should involve both individual activity and a constructive sharing of ideas.

Economies are often applied to some of these activities, for reasons variously of principle, examination pressures, restricted facilities, or teachers' work-load, but the reasons for such economy rarely withstand close inspection. Under the worst state of economic siege which can threaten Shakespeare teaching, it may come to consist of *discussion* which is not teacher-led but teacher-governed, and summed up in dictated notes, followed by writing of occasional essays, some of them 'timed', to see whether students can transfer the notes into examinable merchandise. In these conditions *open discussion* will be attenuated, and with it the space for disagreement, uncertainty and speculation which are crucial to exploring Shakespeare. Enactment will be omitted. This may supposedly be for 'lack of facilities'. Admittedly, a drama studio liberates teaching enormously, but if this is not available an ordinary classroom is adequate for many valuable experiments. It may be for 'lack of time'. But the time which is undeniably needed for enactment work is outweighed by the *multiple* learning it permits. In dramatic exploration you are rarely doing only one thing at once, and to doubt pupils' capacity to profit from such work is to underestimate the stimulus to memory and understanding which is given by intense and connected learning experiences. In any case, I know of no answer to the naïve, absolute question: 'How can you understand Shakespearean drama unless you meet it not only as Shakespeare but as drama?' As for *writing*, it is disturbing to find how little written work many A level English candidates actually do. Success at A level depends not on being able to write answers to specific anticipated questions but on being able to write, period: and you learn to write by writing.

It is the central argument of this article, therefore, that if students approach a Shakespeare play in the way most likely to give them enjoyment and a deepening insight, and if they are asked to express that insight through activities which also exercise generally applicable skills, they will be *better* placed than otherwise to deal with examinations. Whether or not it is true of driving tests, it is true of A level Shakespeare work that the examination is not *necessarily* incompatible with art, skill and enjoyment, only that it can easily be made so.

'Progressive integration' is the core of the teaching strategy I am advocating, and I shall shortly try to exemplify it through one or two particular instances. First, however, it may be useful to set my outline against a summary undertaking of the same kind in an article by Brian Rowe, which discusses Shakespeare teaching (not solely at A level) under the heading 'What are we trying to achieve?' He writes:

'Some of the reasons for teaching and examining Shakespeare at C.S.E. and G.C.E. 'O' and 'A' Levels can be put in the following order of importance:

1) Response to and analysis of situations (e.g. the deposition scene in *Richard II*).

2) Response to and analysis of characters (e.g. Falstaff).

3) Dramatic experience (e.g. the reasons for the Porter's speech or the long Act IV scene ii in *Macbeth*).

4) Poetic experience (e.g. The Queen Mab speech in *Romeo and Juliet*).

5) Literary skills (e.g. analysis, discussion and essay writing on a Shakespearean topic).

6) Analysis and understanding of Elizabethan society and ethics (e.g. the concept of kingship in *Henry V*).

7) Theatre history (e.g. The Globe and how its form affected the shape of Shakespeare's plays).

8) Language study (e.g. semantic development since Shakespeare's death, e.g. 'still', 'presently', 'power').

9) Philosophic experience (e.g. the concept of 'tragedy', 'romance').

Some of these aspects may occur at the same time and some may have more priority with one teacher than with another . . . some may not be possible or desirable until the Sixth Form stage.'[1]

In many respects this will probably seem a more familiar and more achievable agenda than the one I am proposing, and there are substantial areas of attention where we overlap. I quote it because it is representative. Taking the overlaps as self-evident, it may be helpful to emphasise where, as a policy for Shakespeare teaching, my own approach differs from it. This may illuminate what I mean by 'progressive integration'.

The 'reasons' are presented as if they all had *intrinsic* value (though not equal importance). Some clearly do. Most, however, have a usefulness which is chiefly contextual, dependent on full experience of the play itself. Brian Rowe's programme shows the tendency of Shakespeare teaching to split up into a variety of constituent activities, insufficiently connected with each other and tending to acquire an arbitrary value of their own, almost independent of their Shakespearean prompting. What is listed as 'Language Study' is a case in point. For

84

most A level students there is no inherent purpose in knowing that in Shakespeare 'still' means 'always' or 'presently' means 'immediately', except that it allows us to read Shakespeare more accurately. At A level the evolution of linguistic meaning is not an important topic in its own right. It is an obstacle we have to negotiate, a quickly diminishing nuisance. True 'language study' involves something much richer and more extensive. The same point applies to 'Theatre history'. It is of minor importance as general knowledge, especially since Shakespeare's plays have proved themselves capable of untroubled adaptation to centuries of changing theatre architecture; it matters at A level only if it provides specific insights into individual plays.

Fragmentation of knowledge *about* plays is coupled with fragmentary approaches to the plays themselves. For example, what is termed 'Poetic experience' suffers by detachment from context. The Queen Mab speech is not a poem but a speech by Mercutio. Its quality of dramatic fantasy is inseparable from him. Through him we perceive its links with the dangerous behavioural extravagance which characterises Shakespeare's Verona. Seeing it as part of a consistent pattern, we can then observe the ironic link between the speech's buoyant loveliness and the tragic social design of the play. To treat it in isolation, as something obviously 'poetic', is to misunderstand it as drama.

It is the tendency of such a programme to substitute piecemeal information *about* plays for integrated experience *of* plays that I would wish to emphasise. It probably accounts for the absence of any reference to theatrical pleasure, or the role of Shakespeare courses in fostering it, and for what I see as an impoverished implicit definition of 'Dramatic experience'. It is certainly important to know the 'reasons for the Porter's speech'. They concern both surface structure and thematic development. But it is also important to know the *effects* of the speech, not only by discussion but by dramatic enactment. Only in this way will students reach dramatic experience, as opposed to literary explanation. The Porter gives the audience a moment of appalled relief, a brief comedy of imagined damnation in the midst of its fierce reality. This is dramatic experience, and reasons alone, needful as they are, will not arrive at it.

Perhaps my basic disagreement with Brian Rowe's programme lies in distrust of the word 'analysis' (which he applies variously to dramatic experience, historical information and literary skill). 'Analysis' implies an attitude and a value. It has its place, but so do words such as 'approach', 'explore', 'experience', 'speculate', 'test'. Unlike 'analysis', all these words suggest the open-ended and indefinite, and this is what Shakespeare asks for. A Shakespeare play is not a corpse. It is a public meeting. In teaching a Shakespeare play we should surely try to enrich the dramatic experience of students, exploring as many as possible of those dramatic strata which I outlined in the first section of this article, and to do so in a teaching context which uses pupils' own skills as widely and as flexibly as may be. Its purpose is fusion of response to the play as a whole, rather than piecemeal attention to its separable parts. If this seems an ambition beyond the practicable grasp of A level students, perhaps we should nerve ourselves to trust them more. Veronica O'Brien has correctly observed:

We are . . . dealing with experience which matters profoundly in the growth of those we are teaching. It is of utmost importance that we should not underestimate the capacity of the young to find themselves in their encounters with the work. Certainly, we have the responsibility of training students to be reasonably articulate about a text set for examination. But that is not the whole of the matter. There is also the more humanly important factor of a growth in consciousness and responsiveness to human experience. That such growth is not measurable does not make it less important. When what lies between us and a class is a great work of art, there needs to be space for what cannot be explicitly stated; an awareness of what cannot be measured, of the fact that in this situation students can see and hear far more than they can express in words.[2]

Approaching the text

In this section I shall try to exemplify in terms of a teaching strategy how the approach to understanding Shakespeare which I set out earlier can be put into practice. I proposed seven possible responses to the question 'What is the purpose of studying Shakespeare at A level?' In what follows I shall try to include those seven responses in a teaching sequence. It happens that in the main example I have chosen, Macbeth's soliloquy before the murder of Duncan (*Macbeth* Act I scene vii 1–28)*, the suggested teaching sequence closely resembles the order of priority in which the purposes of Shakespeare teaching were initially placed. In many instances I do indeed believe that there is a helpful correspondence here between aims and method, but it is a highly flexible one and must be freely adapted to the needs of any particular play, scene, character or speech, and even more so to the needs of each particular group of students. The general principle involves a process of 'closing in and opening out' – moving gradually into a close encounter with a particular 'detail' of text, and then working out to replace it with deepened insight in its full dramatic context. This can be done with a whole scene, or a set of spaced-out appearances by a single character, or many other variations, but in this case the centrepiece is a single major speech. The word 'detail' used above is helpful in that a 'detail' of text can be treated exactly like the 'detail' of a painting – rewarding very close scrutiny but meaningless except as part of a larger composition.

Here, then, is Macbeth's great speech:

If it were done, when 'tis done, then 'twere well
It were done quickly: if th' assassination
Could trammel up the consequence, and catch
With his surcease success; that but this blow
Might be the be-all and the end-all here,
But here, upon this bank and shoal of time,

* All line references are to the Arden Shakespeare edition, edited by Kenneth Muir.

We'd jump the life to come. But in these cases,
We still have judgement here; that we but teach
Bloody instructions, which, being taught, return
To plague th'inventor: this even-handed Justice
Commends th'ingredience of our poison'd chalice
To our own lips. He's here in double trust:
First, as I am his kinsman and his subject,
Strong both against the deed; then, as his host,
Who should against his murtherer shut the
     door,
Not bear the knife myself. Besides, this Duncan
Hath borne his faculties so meek, hath been
So clear in his great office, that his virtues
Will plead like angels, trumpet-tongu'd, against
The deep damnation of his taking-off;
And Pity, like a naked new-born babe,
Striding the blast, or heaven's Cherubins, hors'd
Upon the sightless couriers of the air,
Shall blow the horrid deed in every eye,
That tears shall drown the wind. – I have no
     spur
To prick the sides of my intent, but only
Vaulting ambition, which o'erleaps itself
And falls on th'other –

What follows is one possible way of approaching it.

Stage One The 'naïve' reading of *Macbeth*. If *Macbeth* is
a set play, it should first be read through quickly, aloud,
from start to finish. The teacher should hog the main
parts ruthlessly, to get as smooth and vigorous a reading
as possible, while announcing that he will hand over this
starring role to pupils as soon as they feel ready to take
it on. Probably some or all of the group will already
'know the plot', but the stated purpose at this stage
should be at least to *pretend* otherwise, to put ourselves
in the position of a naïve audience whose first interest
is in the sweep of the drama and 'what happens next?'
The teacher can supply prompting clues to focus attention on essentials, but these should be informal and for
fun, aiming at racy first impressions rather than polished

delivery. (Recordings should not be used at this stage. A rough 'do-it-yourself' workshop approach will give a much more productive working atmosphere than passive listening.) This stage roughly corresponds to the principle of 'Shakespeare as theatre, for enjoyment'.

Stage Two Having discussed the play's appeal to a 'naïve' audience, repeat the reading more slowly and consideringly. The purpose this time is to notice the effects of prior audience knowledge, and so to introduce attention to structure and dramatic irony; to pause and discuss the characters as people, not exhaustively or systematically but at moments of significant change; and to deal with speeches where difficult language is felt to be a serious obstacle. Macbeth's speech which begins 'This supernatural soliciting . . .' (1 iii 130–142) is a likely instance. The discussion should combine explanation of difficulties with speculation on *why* the language is difficult. In the case of Macbeth's speech in 1 iii, verbal complexity can be seen as a dramatic statement of shock and the sudden collision of conscious and suppressed impulses. This reading links intermittent detailed study of language with character development and plot structure: it begins to *use* language as a way of penetrating more deeply into what is most naturally interesting, namely people and events. It corresponds to the second phase of approach, where confidence and competence are growing, and reading can support, rather than undermine, performance.

Stage Three With this background, significant 'details' of the text can now be approached, and Macbeth's soliloquy moves out from its dramatic setting to the foreground. At this point our interest is unashamedly in character, and no tradition of critical recoil from Bradley should deflect us. We have in front of us a man in a state of deep indecision, driven by previous temptation and sudden opportunity to the point of doing something which, on the one hand, he badly wants to achieve, but on the other hand he knows there are powerful reasons for *not* doing. At this point improvisations rooted in equivalent modern situations can illuminate the universality of Macbeth's plight. He is highly individualised, but he is also the type of all men and women who are torn between conscience and motive, or who can only match themselves with a prized ideal by violating the ideal itself, or whose very opportunism heightens the anguish of indecision. The emphasis here, as in the third suggested approach, is to test character through predicament.

Stage Four This relates character and predicament to personal and absolute morality, and in this process is bound to ask whether *absolute* morality exists. As Macbeth tries to reason himself out of ambitious desire, we can look at the reasons he advances for abandoning the murder-scheme, and ask ourselves how far they are the product of a particular system of values in a particular culture (in other words, what they tell us about Macbeth's Scotland and, by inference, about Shakespeare's England) and how far they might claim absolute, exceptionless validity for all men at all times. This is no light matter: one way in which Shakespeare is our contemporary is that, like us, he faces the ultimate question of what happens when you bend the absolute.

This in turn leads us to consider the facts of Macbeth's moral dilemma and ask, at the other extreme, whether it is entirely or primarily a *moral* dilemma at all. In short, we should ask the simple question, 'What reasons does Macbeth give for *not* committing the murder?' The answer, even in summary, is interesting. There are reasons of pure selfish practicality ('I might get found out', 'Ambition is often self-defeating'). There are reasons which rest on the absolute imperatives of a culture (Macbeth is Duncan's 'kinsman', 'subject', 'host'). There is a reason which rests on personal moral valuing (Duncan is not only king, but a *good* king). The thought of Duncan's goodness seems to spur a further move towards *absolute* prohibition (murder, almost independently of its victim's nature, is a 'horrid deed').

In this way the perspective of absolute and relative morality merges inextricably with individual psychology. This merging gains further complexity if we ask whether the mere fact that Macbeth is assembling, accumulating, *listing* reasons (without our denying for a moment their emotional charge) does not itself arouse suspicion. A vast collection of differently-based reasons is perhaps less convincing than just one. (An interesting parallel to illustrate this point can be drawn with Donne's sonnet 'Death be not proud', an act of ostensibly triumphant poetic defiance which powerfully communicates the very fear it dismisses, and does so by its desperate aggregation of diverse arguments.)

Stage Five This involves a close study of language as action. I do not mean that comment on Macbeth's dramatic language should be deliberately postponed until now: it should receive attention as it is called for at any point by – for example – differences of psychological interpretation or experiments in comparative enactment. But at this stage pupils should be well placed to test moral and psychological conclusions or likely performance effects against details of style. One or two instances will suffice to illustrate this. If Macbeth is reasoning himself out of powerful temptation, the contorted syntax and clustered sibilants of the opening lines may verbally enact a desire for *closure*, an effort to shut within painful, brief finality of language the brief finality of murderous action which he longs for but distrusts: the condensed verbal effort (like in due course the act of murder itself) is a tortured failure. Again, the imagery of eyes, sight and tears in lines 23–25 powerfully combines personal revulsion from an imagined spectacle of murder with fear of its exposure, and of the anguished condemnation it will bring. (Both ideas are developed later: see 2 ii 50–1 and 58, and 2 iii 72–3; such correspondences are part of the 'opening-out' from close textual alertness, and bring insights unattainable without it.)

Stage Six This carries the inquiry out beyond textual detail, and immediate questions of moral psychology, to the huge questions of fate, predestination, and the workings of the supernatural. Discussion initiated at this point will ultimately lead to the great, unavoidable question, 'Why is Macbeth, who is indisputably evil, a tragic hero?' The answer to that question must first negotiate such problems as 'Do the witches have external and fateful reality, or are they dramatic embodiments of irresistible forces within Macbeth himself?' But they can be approached here and now, with another of the 'naïve' questions that should scarcely ever be avoided: 'Why does Macbeth, having accumulated such powerful reasons for *not* murdering Duncan, shortly afterwards kill him?' This question will inevitably open out from the soliloquy itself to the scene as a whole, and then into the full context of the play. The simple response is 'Because Lady Macbeth persuades him to.' That this is *not* a simple response can be exposed by asking the students to weigh Lady Macbeth's arguments in the scale against Macbeth's. They will barely tilt it. Clearly it is not a matter of *arguments* at all. Explanation can perhaps stop short at the immediate emotional diagnosis: that Macbeth is overwhelmingly susceptible to any impugning of his manliness and courage. But this will not really work, either: as a trial of courage the situation is incongruous to the point of madness with all the prior tests which have left his honour shining.

There is, I think, no plausible understanding which omits fate. Nor is there one which can separate fate from the human will. If we believe the witches, Macbeth's fate is predestined. If we look at Macbeth, we see him at times when he has a choice, see him struggling, see him choosing. But these are not contradictory facts of experience. We know that life is lived by all of us in two dimensions; the first is spontaneous and linear, so that we *do* make choices, but the second is a potential retrospect, the inevitable moment when the completed life will be an accomplished fact, and it will be possible for others than ourselves to look back across its years and to discover, amongst all its choices and indecisions, a fateful and inexorable logic. (Not for nothing is this like the two dimensions of drama, and the 'naïve' and knowledgeable audience perspectives with which this teaching sequence started). In brief, we cannot understand *Macbeth* without realising that fate and human choice are compatible. That realisation may be achieved by opening out from this speech into the full scene, and observing that in her persuasions Lady Macbeth is at once an ambitious wife and a functionary of fate. It is a fate which is external to Macbeth but also within him, as the close texture of his soliloquy will show. In Middleton and Rowley's *The Changeling*, the evilly persuasive De Flores addresses Beatrice-Joanna, as the external embodiment of her guilt, with lines which epitomise the situation of Macbeth:

> Can you weep fate from its determined
> purpose?
> So soon may you weep me.

Stage Seven This stage, which I have termed 'deep structure', can be approached from the vantage point of this speech and scene also. It is a scene where at first Lady Macbeth seems the firmer in resolution and emotional strength, Macbeth perhaps the more scrupulous. It is an important commonplace of criticism that in the event it is Macbeth who proves the stronger, growing harder with experience of sin, while Lady Macbeth falls prey to scruple and conscience. The first signs of that reversal are observed to be already present in this scene, with Lady Macbeth's

> I have given suck, and know
> How tender 'tis to love the babe that milks me
> (lines 54–5)

already indicating repressed susceptibilities to tenderness. This is all, I think, quite true. Also true, however, and clearly discernible if we examine Macbeth's soliloquy closely and then open out into the play, is the poignancy of tragic marriage which makes *both* of them determine on a self-inflicted (or mutually inflicted) wounding. If Lady Macbeth is seen straining to violate what is deepest in herself, the natural impulses of love and care towards father, husband and child, so Macbeth is seen straining to violate what is deepest in him, the impulses of 'honour, love, obedience' which are expressed in 'host', 'kinsman', 'subject'. The consequence for Lady Macbeth is madness, and for Macbeth despair – which in Shakespeare is always closely akin to madness. Her it brings to sleep-walking and death, him to that moment of most coherent and self-knowing despair:

> ... that which should accompany old age,
> As honour, love, obedience, troops of friends,
> I must not look to have ... (5 iii 24–6)

This is an example of what I term deep structure, and in this section I have tried to show it as the natural outcome of an appropriately structured teaching sequence.

It may be said that the example, a single major speech by a major character, is loaded in favour of such an approach. A contrasting example, then, would be *Antony and Cleopatra*, Act 3 scene i, in which Ventidius and Silius, two relatively insignificant officers of Antony's forces, are shown discussing their local military situation on 'a plain in Syria'. We may ask the question, 'What is this scene for?'

In early readings it will serve a passing but not unimportant purpose in suggesting how *busy* Rome is, how far-flung and multiple its military ventures. It gives a localised, immediate reality to the 'wide arch of the ranged empire'. Its characters are minor, but very shrewd, very prudent, very astute, very *Roman*. They add to the play's depiction of 'Romanness', and their predicament is a Roman one: the need to make accurate political judgments of military success. The moral texture of the scene is thin: its opening morality of revenge is appropriately governed by cold notions of evenness, but morality is otherwise (typically of the play's Rome) subsumed in politics. The language of the scene is businesslike and muted (again appropriately) but not for that reason without interest: on the contrary, its substance is closely concerned with *balance*, with an even-handed, prudent weighing-up of gain and loss, and Ventidius' vocabulary and syntax are scrupulously balanced accordingly. The style is the man, and the man is Roman. A scene which has significant local effects also has wider significance. Through Ventidius we learn something about Antony, and it is the *Roman* Antony, one who is jealous of reputation's sums, whose image is extended.

In the much-canvassed contrast between Rome and Egypt in the play, one aspect which is fundamental and yet curiously under-emphasised is the contrast between Roman meanness and Egyptian prodigality – a contrast which extends to money, food and material advantage, to the intangible capital resources of honour and reputation, and ultimately to life itself. We are very accustomed, both directly and by report, to the spendthrift Egyptian Antony, but have fewer indirect suggestions of his Roman parsimony, especially when, as here, he participates in his nation's cold absurdity of measuring the unmeasurable. Through Ventidius, in this little, arbitrary, 'dispensable' scene in Syria, the imaginative range of the whole play is stretched. The geography of Empire serves a multiple thematic purpose. Different as this scene is from that in *Macbeth*, it is likeliest to yield its full substance to a comparable teaching approach.

'Ideally, perhaps, the practical and critical study of a play should go hand in hand.'[3] In this account I have assumed that the 'activities' mentioned earlier will take place. Study of this kind cannot be profitably undertaken without an approach through drama which includes improvisation and enactment. It also needs a varied approach through discussion which includes, for example, a forum in which critical viewpoints are presented and compared by pupil-advocates, who will learn in the process how to use the critics critically. And the approach through writing should include full-scale projects (if possible co-operatively prepared) as well as production notes for scenes and other variations on second-hand critical essays. Such activities take time, of course, but they also *save* time. They are not, or need not be, a luxury before the real A level grind gets started; rather they are a direct road to examination competence, a way of seriously combining the examination requirement with the Shakespearean experience, of matching means with ends.

An approach of this kind serves the essential purpose which all teachers of Shakespeare at this level, whatever teaching style they opt for, need to keep in mind. The examination result which the sixth former gains is a collaborative one, even though we treat it as the pupil's own. We tacitly admit its collaborative nature when we assess a teacher's performance by the results which pupils achieve. The nature of that collaboration varies widely, from shameless coaching and cramming to an approach which fosters a satisfying independent confidence in the pupil. Making such independence possible is a harder teaching task than cautious exam drilling, and a more unnerving one. Teachers can scarcely be blamed for playing safe. But the argument of this article is that an approach on the teacher's part which both takes and offers responsibility is not risky, and is likely to produce exam results which are not only more meaningful, but better, than those which emerge when the teacher is a surrogate examinee, twenty times over. The teacher takes responsibility for the sequenced teaching of the text, but passes responsibility for *response* to the pupils, through a broad range of challenging expressive activities. In this way, effective exam preparation can be combined with the essential purpose of the work, which is to pass Shakespeare into our pupils' own possession, not only for the duration of the exam but for life. All the subsidiary uses of A level are discredited if we do not attend to that.

NOTES

1 Brian Rowe, 'Teaching Shakespeare in the Secondary School', in *English in Education*, Volume 13 (1979) no 2, p 44.

2 Veronica O'Brien, *Teaching Shakespeare*, Arnold, 1982, p. 58.

3 *Drama: Education Survey 2*, H.M.S.O., 1967, p. 24.

Circe and the Cyclops:
A Shakespearean Adventure[1]

JOHN SAUNDERS

Do we always have to test understanding and appreciation of Shakespeare – surely the most 'writerly' of dramatists – by the essay, often a most unreadable form for presenting 'readerly' readings?[2]

I say 'often'. There are two ways of writing about Shakespeare. The Circean tradition, bringing to the texts something of the imaginative vision of a good production, works through enchantment and creative metamorphosis. Though sometimes pig-headed – Jan Kott on *A Midsummer Night's Dream*, perhaps – the readings are always alive and interesting. The Cyclopean is a dead tradition. Its practitioners destroy, devour and regurgitate. If not blind, they tend to be one-eyed.

Much of the writing about Shakespeare produced by students in higher education is of the latter kind. In the words of the recently published manifesto of the *Association for Visual Arts*:

> Students of English at polytechnics and universities often write dull, second-hand discursive prose and are taught to do nothing else.[3]

The manifesto is a remarkable document. It marks the moment when a number of lecturers in higher education – some very distinguished – came out of their caves.

What follows is an account of an experiment in encouraging students to write about Shakespeare in modes other than the formal essay – modes which require imaginative and essentially playful engagement with texts.[4] Though given impetus by recent developments in University English teaching which are discussed later in this paper, the experiment began somewhat apologetically several years ago when, fresh from marking O level, I was struck by the contrast between the vitality of some of the work produced by sixteen-year-olds and the 'dull, second-hand discursive prose' being written by their future teachers.

The O level answers whose vitality had impressed me tended to result from questions which asked for a response in the form of a letter, a diary, a newspaper article or a scene from a play. Here are a few examples:

As You Like It
Write two letters, one from Jaques and one from Audrey, each giving an impression of the happenings in Arden.

The Taming of the Shrew
Write the diary entry that Bianca might have made, reflecting on love and marriage, on the night of her wedding.

A Midsummer Night's Dream
Write a scene from 'Bottom's Dream', the work which Quince decided to write following the success of 'Pyramus and Thisbe'.

Questions like these have been a feature of the Oxford and Cambridge Schools Examination Board for many years and are now not confined to this board.[5] They have not always proved popular with teachers, who every year challenge their appropriateness and value in literature papers. Arguments against their inclusion have included the following: they tend to trivialise literature; they demand too subjective a response; they are impossible to assess; they indicate that the setters have not read 'How Many Children Had Lady Macbeth?'! However, they have become increasingly popular with examiners, and especially senior examiners. The reason for this is simple. Whereas most O level literature questions, however provocative, tend to produce answers of a Cyclopean kind – behind which Brodie's or the teacher's notes are a clearly discernible palimpsest – these more unconventional questions can produce lively and inventive responses from candidates who have elsewhere given no glimmers of enjoyment, involvement in the text, or individual insight.

Could the sclerosis which seemed to characterise so much of the work I found myself marking when I began teaching in higher education be arrested by offering students opportunities to try their hands at more creative responses? When one of my teaching commitments became a B.Ed. Honours Shakespeare option I determined to experiment. The teaching conditions were in many ways ideal. I had 90 minutes per week with a small, enthusiastic group who had all chosen to study Shakespeare, rather than parallel options on aspects of Modern literature. The students, by that time in their fourth year, regarded the academic focus of their degree as rather remote from the work they would soon be involved in as teachers and it was easy to persuade them to devote time and energy to forms of writing other than the essay.

Initially the results were disappointing. Not all O level candidates respond imaginatively to imaginative questions. Some produce conscientious, dull narrations, and my first batch of Honours students were very similar. Their 'Ophelia's diaries' were conscientious but quite untouched by imagination. There was no attempt to explore feelings beneath formal statements or to place themselves in an imagined Ophelia's situation in scenes where she is silent or to allow the imagined play to overflow the boundaries of the text. All were dutiful and syntactically pure, even in madness and death. Looking back, the poverty of invention was predictable. The students concerned were all competent essay writers but in need of remedial assistance when it came to using their own imaginations. They were the relatively successful heirs of a tradition which had set out to inhibit all forms of subjectivity. After all, mocking Bradley's unliterary speculations was still an integral part of the very same Shakespeare course in which I was trying to encourage them to imagine!

The following year I determined to be a little bolder. Three weeks were set aside for a highly subjective exploration of *As You Like It*. A full session was devoted to creating an imagined life within and beyond the text. We played analogy games, casting the play from public figures and sets of friends and trying to find contemporary situations and settings. Perhaps more effectively, we took the action at key moments and attempted to explore the sub-textual feelings of both major and minor characters. What might the Duke feel at the prospect of re-gaining a kingdom but losing a daughter? Does Phebe's final couplet carry with it her conviction? What might Jaques think and feel as he sets out to join Duke Frederick? Why is Adam silent? Participants were encouraged to see the text as a magic mirror through which they could pass into an imaginative world of their own creation. Following several exercises like this, I asked the group to spend a week writing letters from a character or characters looking back on Arden, and suggested that they might like to read *The Sea and the Mirror* and attempt to develop their letters into a poem cycle. The results were much more interesting. Before looking at passages from two of the responses brought to the first workshop, it should be noted that all participants remarked on how the assignment had made them read and re-read the play – a form of preparation apparently not always forced upon them by my seminars or their formal essays! Here are three poems from a six-poem cycle called *Looking Back on Arden*:

Adam Afterwards

The forest is strangely songed
By flights of wind-breezed laughter
Caught in a time without memory;
I am the forgotten past and to come.
   Thinking only of their love
   They dance back to the world.

The forest is strangely silent.
It has forgotten the lovers' song.
A leaf settles on the abandoned feast,
And a deer feeds by the stream.
  Longing for a shadowy sleep
  I stumble forward into the depths.

Sir Oliver Martext's Confession

My part in life was very small –
Thirty-six words, four lines in all –
And HOURS to wait for the curtain call!

Jaques

I stand in melancholy stillness, here
At the heart of the oak and watch you play
Blind Man's Buff, day after timeless day –
You do not see my shadow lurking near
Turning my lump of lust in your joy's song,
Feeding my pain with the sublime thought
That you dance the measured step of this world's
  time

And to this world you still in time belong;
And when the game is over, the blind eye
Will see the dark centre of the forest's bone.

  I am a creature of nowhere and know
  To run the arrow singing from the bow.

Although consciously aware of the limits of a make-believe world, this cycle is in essence a celebration, whose images, rhythm and tone encourage the reader to remain within or to re-enter the imaginary world of the play. The next response is in the form of a letter written from Celia to Jaques which, while, I think, still developing energies within the original, sets out to satirise *As You Like It*, the space between the imagined and the real and the conventions of romantic comedy. Somewhere behind its genesis, I suspect, lies Stoppard's *Rosencrantz and Guildenstern are Dead*. Unfortunately, restrictions of space do not allow for the printing of the whole letter. Here is the final section:

from *Dear Jaques*

.... There was a low moaning coming from Orlando's apartment occasionally punctuated by the high pitched hyena cackles from Rosalind's. Charles investigated the former and discovered Orlando stretched out on his bed, weeping like a baby, and, you won't believe it, dressed in the self–same garb. There was no need for Charles to ask the reason – the poor baby leapt at the opportunity for confession. Rosalind, ever one for strange capers, and frustrated by the rumours at large and the stricter court watch, had taken to refusing her husband his rights and duties. Though an ox in most ways, it would seem that Orlando has become something of a stallion in others. Imagine his predicament when his erstwhile playful mare refused him all unless he agreed to a change in roles. This explains the furtive order carried out by Charles. Alas, it would seem that, even as a princess, Orlando was not to suffice. But this is by no means the end of Rosalind's saga. We are indebted to an even older friend of Audrey's for the next episode.

Do you remember William, the quite remarkably simple boy who was best man at Audrey's wedding? Well, William has written to tell us the news in the forest. It was a long letter, full of boring, illiterate detail, but it contained some significant pieces of scandal. It centred on the fate of Silvius and Phebe – the couple whom we decided were a kind of parody of pastoral yokels. Apparently their nuptial voyage lasted even less long than Touchstone's and Audrey's. Poor Silvius died on his honeymoon – a victim not of love but of food poisoning. There were allegations and accusations but Phebe's mother swayed the jury by claiming that Silvius had received his just deserts by trapping into wedlock a girl whose innocence of real life had led her into a number of confusions – of which the difference between a mushroom and a toadstool was a minor one. Phebe was acquitted, but shortly afterwards received a summons to appear at court. She went fearing that the case had been re-opened but received, to her and her mother's amazement, an offer from the Duke of a life pension on condition that she become the Princess's lady's maid.

We had then heard nothing of this at court but through Audrey rumours soon found a way. The Duke had tried to cover up the whole affair. But some courtiers, taking advantage of his leniency (and I suspect really eager to change well-meaning ineffectuality for the cold efficiency of my own father), had apparently demanded a public enquiry. When the Duke dealt with them with unaccustomed severity they unleashed a new rumour – 'like daughter, like father' they said. And I think that many people now really do believe that that fleeting of Time in the Golden world was not all innocence. It's nonsense, of course, though I must say I could never understand why he didn't remarry when my Aunt died and why he always preferred the company of younger men. That Amiens, for instance – a nice enough fellow but more like a girl than a boy. And even now he seems most at home in the set of that effeminate Le Beau. However, I digress.

Dear Jaques, as things have turned out you were so right. We were all so won over by Spring and youth and freedom and lack of responsibility. But who would have thought that April would give way so quickly to December? And even you, dear, wordly, cynical old Jaques could not have anticipated the outcome. The art form of the moment here is something called 'tragi-comedy'. It is a kind of attempt to rationalise the bastard form of drama which has always been with us. The basic idea is that the themes and actions are potentially tragic but that they move towards a comic resolution. As so often happens, art is at variance with nature. For here, though the setting a week ago seemed ripe for your invective, a satirist's dream, who could have suspected that it would all end in death? Not one death but two.

The first to go was poor Orlando. Love–sick, spurned, forlorn, he took again to writing verses and wandering about in a state of melancholic disarray, unshaven and half–dressed. His eyes took on a kind of madness. I found him wandering through our orchard two days ago and should have realised the potential danger. But who could have guessed that the next day Touchstone would find him drowned at the bottom of the pond? To make it more embarrassing, this time he was fully dressed – skirt, smock, bonnet and a complete array of underwear. What these tailors won't do for money!

The court was agog and the revolutionary party demanded an embassy to be sent to my father. Our house was plagued by unofficial ambassadors endeavouring to win my confidence. But I was never all that fond of Dad and certainly have no desire to return to the palace. Oliver may be a bore, but he is normal.

The culmination of the tragedy occurred yesterday. It is really quite unbelievable. Touchstone has been killed in a duel. Apparently some courtier took on himself the fool's office and suggested to Touchstone that he had changed his cap for a pair of horns. They quarrelled. The retort courteous led on to the quip modest and on and on past the retort churlish until they measured swords and Touchstone now lies with Orlando.

Both deaths have been hushed up. The Duke, I suspect, has learned something of government from my father and the last rumour received this morning is of a new party on its way to Arden.

Love,

Celia.

For some readers the excesses of the above passage may be as much reminiscent of Tom Sharpe as Tom

Stoppard. Tom Sharpe was even then proving to some the truth of Wilde's dictum that 'Life imitates Art'. The world of *Wilt*, over–the–top parody for the uninvolved, was becoming a reality for institutes in the process of 'diversification', moving from teacher training to 'real degree work'. CNAA loomed like a presence in a de Chirico painting. Kafka ceased to seem fantastical. The words 'academic rigour' were in the air everywhere. There was a flurry of genuine academic activity – Ph.D.s blossoming like mushrooms – and a greater flurry of pseudo–academic activity as old courses were poured into new bibliographies. Though this rite of passage may have done comparatively little harm to the teachers involved, it can have been of little benefit to the new student intake. Initially, some of these B.A. students lacked both the qualifications to read English at University and the energy and determination to follow a career in teaching. Others had energy and ability but had been very badly taught. As a group they were as appropriate for the new 'academic rigour' as Falstaff's recruits were for Shrewsbury. Lectures, like funeral services, were followed by silent seminars in which the death of the text was mourned. If asked to justify our dreary rituals, many of us would bring out the old arguments that we were the unacknowledged high priests of civilised moral values. The hiatus between such Arnoldian idealism and the students' actual experiences were (and are) too dizzying to contemplate.

Any academic debate in the Senior Common Room tended to be between advocates of the old humanism and the converts to the 'new rigour', generally referred to loosely as 'structuralism'. Often this was a conflict between a group whose professed love of literature was a guiding principle and their adversaries who saw literature as providing material for linguistic, sociological or psychological analysis. The debate unexpectedly became a national one – even featuring in the *Financial Times* – when the English Faculty at Cambridge expressed itself in the MacCabe affair.

In retrospect, the quarrel seems to have centred on the relationship between English and *other* disciplines:

traditionalists arguing for the cultural value of the 'canon' and wanting to preserve links with Greats, History, Religious Studies and other branches of a traditional Humanities curriculum; modern theorists arguing that teachers of Literature have much to learn from the 'more rigorous' new methodologies deriving from Structural linguistics and seeing the study of Literature as a potentially interesting branch of Anthropology, Sociology or Psychoanalysis. But in the Cambridge debate there was one voice which argued eloquently for a very different approach to Literature, paying central allegiance not to the Humanities nor to the Social Sciences but to the Arts. This was how Dr Michael Long saw his ideal University English Faculty:

> I would want to get creative writers here. I would want the live theatre brought into close contact with our drama studies. I would want facilities for the proper study of art forms, such as film and song, where language is only one of the elements.[6]

Within the parameters of the Cambridge debate this may have seemed an eccentric lone voice. But nationally there was a growing movement in universities and other institutes of higher education to free the study of Literature from what, for many, had become a crippling academicism. On 21 October 1983, the *Association for Verbal Arts* published its manifesto declaring that:

> Urgent reforms are needed in the teaching of English, particularly in secondary schools and higher and further education. For most people, training in the verbal arts is a missing subject.[7]

The manifesto urged that English should be regarded as one of the Arts and that in keeping with the traditions of arts such as Music and Painting, *creation, performance* and *practice* should be integral to both teaching and examining. Students of English at all levels – the manifesto suggests – should not be just writing essays about poetry, they should be actively involved in developing skills in reading poetry aloud and in learning to write in a range of verse forms. The manifesto was signed by both academics and professional writers and it had strong support from both the educational left and right. *Critical Quarterly* reprinted it in its 1984 Spring and Summer issue, assisted in hosting the first of the Association's conferences in April and announced that the editors had decided to make articles exploring new approaches to English teaching a regular feature of future editions. The first accounts of experiments in developing new writing courses have already started to appear.

Whereas some of the signatories to the *Association for Verbal Arts'* manifesto would probably like to see new writing courses running alongside a traditionally taught curriculum, others like Peter Abbs and John Broadbent have urged more radical reforms.

Dr Abbs has repeatedly argued that the so-called crisis in English study – which is now leading to the deconstruction of not only texts but whole literature departments – lies not in the emergence of the new theory but in the more time–honoured tradition which has linked the study of Literature to the Humanities rather than the Arts. In his view it is this linking which has resulted in the overvaluing of discursive, analytical modes of enquiry – the essay, the seminar and the lecture – whose assumptions and methodologies are often in direct conflict with the essential nature of the artefacts they are purporting to explain. He advocates new approaches to teaching which will develop 'a thinking within the medium rather than a thinking about the explicit content':

> Rather than using literature as a means to abstract speculation and linear formation it (i.e. an arts approach to literature) would encourage an indwelling in the literary text – in the rhythm, in the metaphor, in the associations, the mood, the texture, the non-discursive energies of the work. Thus the aim would be to bring the student's feelings, sense perceptions, imagination – and the intelligence active in all of these – inside the text in order to comprehend it. What is being asked for is

a refining of the mimetic imagination, an anchoring of thinking in the aesthetic response.

He offers a tentative list of forms which might displace, but not replace, the essay. These include folders of original work, experimental journals, and a variety of approaches to performance.[8]

'Our subject is "creative", playful, but how can we insert that into academic curricula?'[9] asks Professor Broadbent whose distrust of the traditional modes of teaching literature extends beyond their inappropriateness. He sees lectures, seminars and essays as forms whose hidden, ritual effect, if not their purpose, is the domination of the initiates by the initiated. In his view the ideology of the teaching mode is likely to be more insidious than the ideological content of that being taught. One way of inserting the creative and the playful into the curriculum is, of course, to develop more creative and playful modes of teaching. In so doing, the teacher should be discovering ways of using, rather than suppressing, the energy of the group. John Broadbent advocates teaching methods which will assist students to become more aware of both structure and subjectivity, the formal aspects of literature and the ways in which text and readers meet to create meanings. Like Peter Abbs, he stresses the value of performance, especially performances which provide space for the creative energy of individuals or groups to explore fantasy or to challenge the ideology of received texts and interpretations.

Ideas like these have provided a new impetus and a more secure frame of reference for my more recent teaching. Now three weeks of a course can be devoted to encouraging new modes of writing without the justification that the workshop participants might one day be requiring similar exercises from their pupils. I have become less nervous about possible irrelevance and more interested in the imaginative processes which occur between the reading of a text and the writing of a poem – processes which repeatedly illuminate aspects of meaning seldom recognised in the traditional essay.[10] The next four poems all grew out of a short unit of work on *A Midsummer Night's Dream* and have been chosen to illustrate something of the range of work which one text has provoked and inspired. In the first, Oberon gets his come–uppance in a witty and imaginative reflection on the events following the action of the play.

Titania's Revenge

The peaceful moonlit night
Flees from a bright new day.
TITANIA awakes
And screams the sun away.
Her sweet young Indian boy
To Oberon belongs.
Her waking mind reveals
A catalogue of wrongs.
Lulled by the sweet air
And spells rather than charms,
Her tiny mind forgave
Her lord and all his harms.
'Now that the light reveals
The tricks he played on me
He shall not run and hide
In air, not sky, nor sea.
NOT ALL THE MAGIC IN THIS WOOD
CAN HELP THAT MAN OR DO HIM GOOD.'

Unawares sleeps OBERON,
Wrapped in slumbers deep.
Lying closely next to him
Sleeps a woolly sheep.
The cheerful calling birds
Awake the fairy King.
He looks upon his love
Her praises he doth sing.
IMAGINATION helps
Her seem his own true love.
IMAGINATION can
Turn ravens into doves.
TITANIA steps near
Surveys her hated lord.
Such comedy she knows

Is sharper than a sword.
So let spectators laugh
At shame and love and spite,
For in a fairy's mind
Two wrongs DO make a right.
DREAM OF REVENGE WHILE IN YOUR BED
AND FAIRIES WILL CONTROL YOUR HEAD.

It would be difficult to translate the point of view shown here into the form of a traditional essay without appearing pompous and insensitive. By responding to a possibly uncomfortable aspect of the underlying ideology of the play with imaginative energy and humour, the poem both satirises masculine complacency and, fittingly, celebrates the power of imagination.

The next poem might be crudely categorised as 'psychological'. It is, in fact, an attempt to relate Jan Kott's controversial essay to the play in an imaginative, rather than an analytical, way.

Titania's Dream

I dream of falling trees in wildest storms
Alone I brace myself 'gainst things that fright
And do me harm. The boar with bristled hair,
The ounce I dreamed of once, are here somewhere –
I only sense their presence. Bats that bite,
Beetles, cockroaches and newts and blindworms;
These and other horrors all surround me
But I am blind to everything around me.

What magic keeps my eyes closed through this
    night?
There are such wondrous pictures in my mind:
My love is huge and dark, his muzzle rat-like,
He comes to me with claws, not hooves,
    stretched cat-like.
He's near, my black love, near though I'm still
    blind.
So long sleep I, the moon has bleached me white.
I'll reach for him and stroke his hairy ears
And kiss his open mouth, wet with my tears.

This poem was written for a course where students study a number of texts which, directly or indirectly, explore aspects of the literary imagination. Time is provided for workshops in which poems are submitted for discussion before being re-drafted. Passages offered for discussion can grow directly from the central texts but can also be quite independent. Often the parent text has provided an incidental, rather than a central, focus, as in the two poems which follow. The first is rooted in memory, fantasy and *A Midsummer Night's Dream* and might be regarded as an example of the kind of inter-textuality referred to by Peter Abbs, where a text is absorbed into 'the creative form-seeking life of the psyche'. Here is the fourth and final draft:

Such Shaping Fantasies

He sat by the pattern
of an Italian lake,
criss-crossed with jasmine
in the trellised shadows,
while coffee wreathed
a responsibility to remember,
a scent to steam the stars
on a clear night sometime –
sometime . . .

He walked on the mountains
of the Haute Savoie
in thin green air,
sublimity breathed into touch
among heartsease clinging
to a short summer,
bringing love-in-idleness
to eyelids shutting dreams
into the top of the world –
or should have walked . . .

He lay with me only
when I slept
(white sheets, dark room
and the fear of intrusion)

111

and filtered into photographs
of empty journeys,
holidays taken from
a sense of duty
without exploration.

I have accepted your offer
to make tangible
the shapes of imagination
in a waking pact,
but tell me if fancy blesses:
when I come to you
on our wedding night
(on a clear night sometime, love)
Will he be there?

Some readers have found this poem very difficult. *A Midsummer Night's Dream* holds the key. The persona of the poem remembers her adolescent encounters with an Oberon figure and now, about to marry, muses – will marriage and maturity bring about an exorcism of 'fantasy'?

At the moment of my writing, the sonnet which follows has not yet been discussed in a workshop and may not in the mind of its creator be linked to *A Midsummer Night's Dream* at all. However, when it is discussed, the shared experience of the play will provide a unifying focus. Workshop participants are likely to be more interested in its ambiguities and obscurities and the endeavour to relate the poem to the play will do something towards enriching both. The relationship between the texts might be compared to the relationship between a myth and its literary re-statement.

Cuts and Tears

Lunar pulse and pull, in the pant of night,
Mrs Smith is a sorceress again,
her eyes are full moons, blessed with silver sight,
she spies a god whose faith is on the wane.
Drawn from one crucible, they are moving
towards the tubers. A nagging need throbs

112

in the very jugulars of wrinkling
Beech and runny Spruce. Reality cuts
and tears, carelessly, like some star crazed wolves
whose impulses are to inspirit and claw
at the thin, fraying silks that are themselves.
They are dancing now, binding every flaw
with the belief in what they know to be
and not what others only dimly see.

The course from which these last poems have emerged is a part of the Literature component within the West Sussex Institute's newly–formed 'Related Arts' degree. The relative success of exercises like these, where individuals and groups spend some of their time working on imaginative, rather than analytical, responses to texts, has led to a distinctive feature of the way in which the English work is examined. In place of one of the formal examinations at the end of the degree, students majoring in Literature are given an option in which they can spend two weeks on a creative project linked to a prescribed text. Last year the first intake of students completed their degree and those specialising in Literature all chose this creative mode. They were given *Twelfth Night* as their text and required to: 'Write a poem cycle in which the principal characters reflect back on the play's action, its themes, its illusions and its ironies.' All submissions proved interesting. One was quite remarkable – a highly polished, consciously formal piece of literary pastiche. The author had begun by selecting forms which she thought appropriate for each of her central characters. So, for example, Olivia's obsessive ecstasy is expressed through a villanelle, Orsino's romantic but rather formal self-indulgence in ottava rima and Viola's intelligent feeling through a sonnet. Other pairings were as follows:

Malvolio: sicilian octave	Sir Andrew: rondolet
Feste: ballad	Sir Toby: triolet
Sebastian: terza rima	Maria: virelay

In addition to the nine main poems, Antonio (a conscious

113

echo of *The Sea and the Mirror*) introduces, links and ends the cycle with ten kyrielles. Space does not allow for printing the complete cycle. Here is a fragment:

Olivia

I taught my love to dance today
beneath the lonely garlanding,
and heard the answering music play.

In winter's soft cathedral grey,
where reason mourned its echoing,
I taught my love to dance today.

And in the west-door, far away,
a heart of light stood questioning,
and heard the answering music play.

Around the light I wove my way,
and in the tracing of the ring,
I taught my love to dance today.

I dared the barren dark to say
that fools should fear the song of spring,
and heard the answering music play.

So, in the brightening season, gay
with garlands green for marrying,
I taught my love to dance today,
and heard the answering music play.

Antonio

That I might find a day when I
see sudden knowledge in the sky,
and set my dancing future free,
O God, keep faith with me.

Orsino

Sing me an old and ancient song, whose rhyme
will celebrate the bone-drummed horse's run,
and beat the passing of a journeyed time
to tell the knight his searching is not done,
and let me hear again the chapel's chime

disturb the air with beauty never won:
for I am legend, ever riding where
you catch in flying dream the snow-white mare.

Sing me an old and ancient song of love,
entwined with roses and with eglantine
that kiss the deepening summer's bower, whereof
the poet writes; and let the song be mine,
that I might repossess the stars above
this slow day's care, and there in Heav'n recline:
for I am Eros, weighted by the earth
in which all flowers of love are dying at birth.

Sing me an old and ancient song, that I
can live again the glory of the chase,
and set my hounds into the whistling sky
to win for me that high and quested race,
and let my favoured huntsmen once more lie
within my own desires and my good grace:
for I am restless, so, boy at my feet,
sing me an old and ancient song my sweet.

The cycle was, in part, the product of the three years' work which had preceded it. In this 'Related Arts' degree Literature is one of four main subjects, the other three being Art, Dance and Music. Students follow introductory courses in all four, before chosing one in which to specialise at the end of their first term. The major subject is then studied within a context where the Arts meet, so that all students, regardless of their specialism, share courses on Modernism, Romanticism and Aesthetics. Main Literature students share a 'Words and Music' course with Music students and a 'Word and Image' course with Art students. Though half the English component is traditional in content, concentrating on the close study of major works, in keeping with the traditions of the other arts, practice (in both performing and writing) is integral to all courses. The more experimental courses are planned to develop insight into literary form and imaginative process through the development of the students' own writing. So, for example, in a first year course, 'Theme and Form in Poetry', students are encouraged to write, first freely then within a variety of forms ranging from haiku to sonnet. A course on 'Modern Drama' is assessed both by formal essay and by literary parody (e.g. 'Write a third act for *Waiting for Godot*') – a form of assessment which is generally found to be challenging and more rewarding than the essay as a means of appreciating a dramatist's craft. In a course on 'Literature and Film', half a term is devoted to studying and practising ways of structuring narrative in film and fiction. Later, a detailed study of Kozintsev's *King Lear* considers both the finished film and the subjective process of 'translation' (well documented in *The Space of Tragedy*), a unit of work which is followed by an opportunity for students to explore their own ideas in translating a text into visual images. In their final year, Literature students follow the course on the 'Literary Imagination' which has already been mentioned.

This paper began as an attempt to show that 'creative criticism' is possible beyond O level and that it is a particularly appropriate means of exploring responses to Shakespeare of a kind which could be expressed only crudely in the traditional essay form. I am reluctant to dwell at any length on teaching method – especially since approaches which succeed with one group may fail dismally with another. More important than a precise methodology is, as I hope the previous paragraph indicates, the overall context in which Literature is studied. If a course on Shakespeare is taught in a degree where lectures and seminars predominate, workshop approaches can produce negative reactions. Where students have had little incentive from O level to the final year of their Honours degree to write in any form other than the essay, the opportunity to write a poem or a poem cycle is likely to be treated with suspicion. It is warm in the cave.

NOTES
1 This chapter is a re-working of an article which is printed in the 1985 Summer issue of *Critical Quarterly*.

Circe and the Cyclops: A Shakespearean Adventure

2 The distinction between 'writerly' and 'readerly' texts is, of course, Barthes'. See Roland Barthes, *S/Z*, (translated by Richard Miller), Hill and Wang, New York, 1974. 'Writerly' texts appeal to the imagination and inventiveness of a reader who, in giving a text an interpretation, in effect re-writes it. 'Readerly' texts do not require creative responses from their readers who, like the Cyclops, become mere 'consumers'.

3 The manifesto was first printed in *The Times Higher Educational Supplement* on 21 October 1983.

4 The best O and A level essays show how the traditional essay form can be used effectively to communicate an imaginative reading of a text. The Circean increasingly gives way to the Cyclopean as writing about Shakespeare becomes more and more advanced. Stanislavsky's 'magic if', can, given imaginative teaching, lead to excellent work for GCE but it is seldom the gateway to a doctorate.

5 John Cox, 'Criticism and creativity in the sixth form', *Critical Quarterly*, vol. 26 nos 1 and 2, 1984, discusses the effectiveness of questions similar to these which are now a feature of the Cambridge Board, lamenting their absence from A level papers.

6 *Cambridge University Reporter*, vol. CXI, no. 18, 18 February 1981.

7 See 3 above.

8 The quoted passage is taken from 'The meaning of English within the arts', *Critical Quarterly*, vol. 26, nos 1 and 2, 1984. See also, in particular, *English within the Arts*, Hodder, 1982.

9 From the 'Workshop Programme', DUET 2. (DUET – Developing University English Teaching – is a project, initiated by Professor Broadbent, which holds an annual workshop at the University of East Anglia for teachers of English and related subjects in higher education.) 'New university English', an earlier statement of Professor Broadbent's theory and practice is available in *Experience in English Teaching*, (edited by David Craig and Margot Heinemann), Edward Arnold, 1976.

10 In *Discovering Shakespeare*, Macmillan, 1981, Professor John Russell Brown recognises the importance of giving freedom to subjective responses to Shakespeare: 'An exhilarating interplay between these elements – Shakespeare's text, its theatrical enactment and our own thoughts and feelings – can transport us into a fabulous world, full of surprises and deep pleasures.' Such journeys can be charted only clumsily, if at all, in an essay.

Active Reading:
Shakespeare's Stagecraft

PETER REYNOLDS

When I was a child, I was lucky enough to *see* Shakespeare before I read him. Almost the whole of my junior school took over the local cinema for a matinée performance of Laurence Olivier's film of *Richard III*. It was altogether a memorable occasion. From the moment George Morris let us into the Regal – he was its manager and a man who excited much speculation and curiosity because he wore a dinner jacket and lived in a caravan – to the time we emerged into the gathering gloom, I experienced something altogether superior to school. Many of the images from that film remain in my head: Richard 'wooing' Lady Anne, Richard on his white horse, Richard finally submerged under the swords of his adversaries – a shot like some mad dance created by Busby Berkley. These stage-pictures have persisted long after most literary critical evaluations of this play have vanished from my mind back on to the library shelves from whence they came.

Please do not misunderstand me; I do not underestimate the importance of literary criticism for teachers and the taught. Indeed, traditional critical approaches to Shakespeare that explore character, theme, images, and so on, are vital tools which begin to open up the printed text. But once that process has begun it needs to be taken a stage further. Both teachers and students must accept, and increasingly many do, that the modern edition of a play by Shakespeare is incomplete and partial without the dimension of performance, be it imagined or practically realised. Of course, it is impossible for anyone to pick up a copy of a play and read it without on some level recreating the events it relates in the imagination. This is a natural and instinctive response, but, because it is natural and instinctive, it tends to be taken for granted and not subjected to careful critical scrutiny.

In my own teaching, I try to tap some of the enthusiasm and imaginative energy that is released when young people actually participate in performance. This is done by encouraging them to develop a critical approach to the act of reading that is both more aware, and more informed about the judgments and decisions being taken (often unconsciously) when dramatic literature is transformed imaginatively into a theatrical event. By stressing that an actual performance is the result of the collaborative effort of many individuals making distinct, but inter-related, texts of their own, you begin to make students realise that they, too, can and should play an *active* part in the manufacture of meaning in the theatre of the mind's eye.

This 'active reading' is a proponent of a basic premise: that an alliance of the intellect and the imagination is necessary to bring a text to life, and that the reader has to *make it happen*. Active reading of a play demands that readers take decisions. First they must try to recognise, and then organise, the huge variety of visual and aural signs that consciously and subliminally are at work making a performance text. They must accept that no single sign, or generator of that sign, be it the gesture of an actor at a particular moment, or a colour used significantly in a designer's setting, is *the* text, but that a performance text is a blend of many different signs and signals. Every collective expression of those signs and signals comprises the play in performance, and each is different from the previous one. Indeed, every witness of a performance sees his own text and not that of his neighbour. That this is so becomes evident from even the most cursory glance at dramatic criticism, let alone from the greatly contrasting discussions of what actually took place, and its significance, that result whenever a lively group of people watch what is purportedly the same performance of a play. Just as each participant in a performance text, and each member of its audience, has to make his or her own text, so students of dramatic literature need to be encouraged to make *their* texts, and these will be the result of the syntheses *they* choose to create after juggling with the different but complementary textual statements which arise during the transition from printed text into performance. This process not only enhances reading and encourages individual non-derivative responses to plays, but also results in a much more satisfactory encounter with the printed text. This is not surprising, for Shakespeare's plays are not intended to be met as poetry hermetically contained between the covers of a book, but to give birth to performances, which necessarily are always first performed on the ideal stage created in the reader's mind.

In my teaching I am not concerned with guiding students towards producing their own plays, but I do attempt to raise the critical status of an approach that acknowledges that the dramatist's printed text is *a* text, not *the* text. It is a starting point for necessary further action. The active reader recognises that actors, directors, designers and audiences, all make their own texts from what has been given them by the dramatist, but know that what they make is *not* the same thing as what has been printed, although the printed text is where the process of interpretation usually starts.

In this essay I want to identify three of the elements present in any performance text, but frequently neglected in more conventional literary, as opposed to dramatic, analysis of Shakespeare's plays: casting, silent characters, and stage properties. In the following active reading of a scene from *Richard III* (1.ii), I hope to illustrate that, if these elements are ignored or omitted, the full text of this extraordinary scene is left un-read.

120

Casting

Casting particular actors and actresses is a task which cannot be avoided in the theatre, and should not be avoided by the active reader of plays. It is, of course, a minefield through which to tread with extreme care, using intuition as well as reason for a guide. It is a process in which subjective judgments and prejudices are rife. Of course, if a dramatist's text indicates clearly and unambiguously that a character possesses specific physical characteristics, then these should be respected. For example, in *A Midsummer Night's Dream*, the actress playing Helena should be taller than the one playing Hermia: the former is referred to as a 'painted maypole' (3.ii 296) and the latter as 'low and little' (3.ii 326). In such an obvious case, the task of casting the roles has partially been done. Rarely is a dramatist so helpful and explicit. As soon as highly subjective terms such as 'beautiful', or 'ugly', or 'plain' are applied to characters in a play, either by the dramatist or by one of the dramatist's characters, then the real issues and problems of casting begin.

When casting a play in the imagination, care must be taken to examine the appropriateness of the immediate images of individual characters which spring to mind. Consideration and reflection often reveal the presence of crude stereotypes. Their origin, nature, and function require exploration. We create these images in our minds' eye whatever we do; the point is consciously and carefully to consider what the imagination offers up as an immediate response to the signals emitted from a dramatist's text. What does, and, in the context of the play as a whole, should, signify 'beauty'? How old is 'old'? Preconceptions must be challenged as we read, and in particular it is necessary to ask how, in the act of casting, we are applying these terms, and to what extent our evidence for their use is reliable and appropriate. To choose a real or an imagined actress or actor for a particular role is to make an interpretative statement about the play. It not only indicates confidence in her or him to perform in a particular way, but also a commitment to an idea of how the character is to be enacted. Casting decisions can affect significantly the overall interpretation of the performance text that will eventually be available to an audience. The active reader has got to think hard about casting.

I mentioned the vivid memory I have of watching Laurence Olivier's film version of *Richard III*. In it, you may recall, he cast himself as Richard, Duke of Gloucester, and, in the minor but significant role of Lady Anne, the young and very beautiful Claire Bloom. One of the most famous scenes in the play, and one of the most memorable in the film, is the so-called 'wooing' scene (1.ii). In Shakespeare's text, Richard is made to confront Anne over the dead body of her father-in-law Henry VI, for whose death he is personally responsible, and whom she is escorting to burial. Richard is also responsible for the death of Anne's husband. She is aware of what Richard has done, but, despite these apparently insurmountable odds, by the end of the scene (less than ten minutes' playing time), Richard appears to have succeeded in winning a promise from her, not only of forgiveness, but also of future love.

Now the scene as Shakespeare wrote it must have appeared to Olivier to be asking far too much of a cinema audience by expecting viewers to believe in the credibility of the action it relates. Indeed, Olivier deliberately exacerbated the potential problems of belief in Richard's actions by changing Shakespeare's text to make the corpse not that of Anne's father-in-law, but that of her husband! What Olivier, a young and highly successful actor and film star, patently wanted to emphasise in *his* text as director and actor, was Richard's ability as a lover: the price was great and much to be desired, and the barriers to its possession enormous. Olivier presumably decided that, to give this scenario a chance of appearing convincing, he had to change what Shakespeare had written. Accordingly, he split the scene into two halves by inserting an earlier episode, in which the hapless Clarence is led off to the Tower, at the point where Anne exhibited the first signs of a change in her attitude to Richard. The break in the scene was obviously intended to lend psychological credibility to Richard and Anne's extraordinary actions. But are these actions really so difficult to accept in performance? Given Shakespeare's text, and not Olivier's, there is, I think, no problem *provided* Lady Anne is properly cast.

Claire Bloom was not only beautiful, she also displayed a strong sense of self-confidence and maturity. But the more impressive the physical presence of the actress playing Anne, the greater will be the audience's difficulty in accepting her seduction as believable and consistent with her character. If you think, for a moment, that this scene shows events at a funeral, you might recall that on such occasions, those most nearly involved with the dead are potentially extremely vulnerable. They may need, and they may seek, consolation where they can find it, for it is an occasion characterised by emotional turmoil and confusion. If you cast in the role of Anne an actress who looks young – perhaps very young, fifteen or sixteen years old – and who is also physically slight and not especially beautiful (we have only Richard's evidence to indicate her physical qualities, and he is hardly the most reliable source), then immediately the actress can begin to articulate a text which displays her vulnerability.

There are other actors in this scene, and we should also consider how to cast them. The corpse is borne on to the stage by pall-bearers and guarded. There are also two silent, but named characters: Tressel and Berkeley. If all these roles are played by tall, powerfully built actors, then what the performance text presents is a contrasting spectacle in which a very young woman is isolated and vulnerable. She is the only woman; she has no apparent allies. Yet this, the least physically impressive person on stage, has the most difficult task to enact. It is *her* difficulty that this casting emphasises; not Richard's difficulty in wooing her. Lady Anne must bury a King, and publicly 'obsequiously lament[ing] Th'untimely fall of virtuous Lancaster.' For Laurence Olivier's Richard successfully to seduce Claire Bloom's Anne in the time given by Shakespeare might well have failed to convince an audience; but, had Olivier's Richard been seen to seduce a near–child at a funeral, the famous soliloquy at the end of the scene, 'was ever woman in this humour wooed? Was ever woman in this humour won?' would have a hollow rather than a victorious ring to it. For what the performance text can show in this scene, if it is appropriately cast, is a conflict in which the eventual 'victory' is negligible because the battle was between vastly unequal forces. This interpretation can be reinforced by careful choice of properties, and by using the large number of silent characters indicated in the printed text.

Silent Characters

When trying to get students to animate a text and to think as actors and actresses, it is useful to remind them that any actor on stage being observed by an audience is acting, irrespective of whether or not he or she happens to be speaking. The significance of this simple fact (that acting is more than talking) is often forgotten when simply reading a dramatist's text. Indeed, when studying the process of how Shakespeare's text becomes a performance it is necessary to remember that the dramatic significance of a character cannot automatically be measured by the number of words he or she is given in the printed text to speak. The active reader has to recall the *context* in which those words are uttered. To do this, he or she must begin by acknowledging the importance for actors of being able to *listen* to other actors speaking. The enactment of listening in a performance can be of equal significance as an expressive act as talking. When reading what the dramatist's text gives character 'A' to say, we cannot fully understand the text by scrutiny, however thorough, of the words being used. We must look to see to whom 'A's' text is addressed. 'B' (the addressee) generates a text through his or her response to what is heard. That reaction, communicated through body-language or gestural action, may well influence what 'A' says, and the manner in which it is said. Although 'A' is speaking the dramatist's text that you can *read*, 'B' is just as significantly articulating a response that you need to *see* in your imagination if you are to begin to understand the complete exchange. Indeed, as far as the audience are concerned, neither of the two actors is speaking *the* text, because that is what the audience themselves are constructing by observing the activity of the two actors and making significance out of it.

The exchange between two characters can, of course, be further complicated when other, perhaps unnamed, characters are also occupying the playing space. In active reading the student must *decide* whether these people are visible to the audience; if they are seen by 'A' or 'B' or by one or neither of them. Can they overhear what is being said by 'A', and is 'A's' text modified as a result? How do those who overhear the discussion react, and how does this reaction further condition and shape the text of the audience? These are factors about so-called silent characters that remind us that they are usually far from silent in terms of the performance text, and also that what is said, and what is meant, do not always correspond. The student who is taught to accept the apparent authority of the written text, and who reads only with the knowledge of the conventions of non-dramatic literature, can all too easily miss many instances of which this is true.

In the 'wooing' scene from *Richard III* we find a good example of the potential power of silent characters to articulate a text, and of the need for the active reader to take positive decisions in order to facilitate a necessary imaginary enactment of that text. The scene presents a classic case of action that cannot be fully comprehended by the reader unless that reader is encouraged to activate his or her imagination and take up the creative challenge offered to it.

In the current Penguin edition of this play, the following stage directions are given for 1 ii:

ENTER THE CORSE OF HENRY VI, WITH HALBERDS TO GUARD IT, LADY ANNE BEING THE MOURNER.

Now the corpse of the dead King (played, presumably, by an actor and not by a dummy) cannot walk on to the stage, and it will therefore need to be carried by at least six actors. The directions specify that the corpse is guarded; it therefore seems reasonable to suppose that those who carry the body are in no position to guard it, and that we therefore require another group of actors to enact the guard. The reader has to decide how many guards guard the funeral procession of a dead King. Shakespeare may have been thinking of the historical evidence contained in Edward Hall's *The Union of the Noble and Illustre Famelies of Lancastre and York*, published in 1584. In this history the funeral of Henry VI is described as a poor affair

> without Priest or Clarke, Torche or Taper,
> syngyn or saiyng . . .

Given this and the relatively small numbers of actors employed by an Elizabethan company, plus the fact that Lady Anne is the only person of rank and status in society to be present, let us suppose that there are six halberds to guard the corpse (not many when you begin to think of state funerals). Although the opening directions don't refer to them, two characters are mentioned by name in the subsequent spoken text: Tressel and Berkeley. These two gentlemen enter with the funeral procession, making a cast of at least sixteen actors on stage at the beginning of the scene: six pall-bearers, six halberds guarding the corpse, Lady Anne, Tressel and Berkeley, and the body of Henry VI. When the actor playing Richard enters the scene you have a stage crowded with seventeen actors, and a printed text that is apparently only concerned with two.

What then is the significance of these figures? How do they enter the playing area, and what impression are they communicating to an audience? What is their collective role in the manufacture of meaning in the performance text? At this point all *I* can do is what I hope *you* will encourage your students to do, in their own ways: that is, to begin to animate the printed text.

Let us say that the procession is formal and solemn. There is no music to accompany the entrance, and the very silence creates an air of expectation and concentration on this strange sight. Lady Anne leads the procession, followed by Tressel and Berkeley, and the corpse, held shoulder–high and closely guarded. It is important to make clear to the audience that control and responsibility for these events lies with Lady Anne. She commands and directs the progress of this funeral rite for a dead King. The corpse appears to be heavy, and the progress across the stage is slow. This gives time for the audience both to note the solemnity of the occasion, and also to register that the only woman on stage (the slight figure of Anne) is ordering events: this impression is confirmed when Anne begins to articulate the first spoken text of the scene with a command 'Set down, set down your honourable load.' As the body of Henry is referred to by Lady Anne throughout the scene, and indeed is used by her as her only defence against the onslaught of Richard's rhetoric, its position on-stage is important. The corpse ought to be physically, as it is metaphorically, central to the action of what follows. The actor playing the corpse is one of the silent characters, but throughout the scene he generates a text that reminds the audience of what Richard has done in the very recent past, the nature of the occasion on which he has chosen to do his 'wooing', and, finally, his lone body prefigures the slaughter still to come.

At Anne's command to set down the corpse, the bearers, guards, and Tressel and Berkeley, apparently cease to have active roles to play in the proceedings and become passive spectators. They are not, however, dramatically passive; they become an on-stage audience which begins to witness Anne's fulfilment of her role in this spectacle: the formal lamentation of 'virtuous Lancaster'. The presence of these fifteen men gives this lament a public quality, and as a public act, a required performance, it carries with it the added stress of responsibility for appropriate behaviour. Up to, and including, this lament, Lady Anne is controlling the progress of the ritual surrounding death. However, immediately Richard enters the stage, her tenuous grasp is loosened and then lost, never to be regained. He takes over management of events, directing and manipulating them according to his own design. Even before Richard enters we can see that Anne is uncertain and tentative. She undermines her own authority by giving an order to the procession to go on, only to countermand it seconds later:

> Come, now towards Chertsey with your holy load,
> Taken from Paul's to be interred there;
> And still as you are weary of this weight,
> Rest you, whiles I lament King Henry's corse.
>
> (129–132)

Richard's entry is so well timed, coming as it does when the bearers are caught with the heavy corpse on their shoulders, uncertain whether to go on or stay, the guards barely ready, and the whole procession yet to regain its impetus and momentum that he may well have been observing the events (visible to the audience perhaps?) and awaiting his opportunity. When he does intervene, the bearers are not sure what to do. Anne has told them to take their 'holy load' up again and, even as they are in the act of so doing, orders them to 'rest'. Richard's opening line, 'Stay you that bear the corse, and set it down', is spoken with authority, as if to intervene on Anne's behalf. It is as if Richard has immediately taken over responsibility for the continuance of the ritual process, and, once this has demonstrably happened, Anne's control of events is critically weakened, just as her self-control will be undermined by Richard's subsequent actions. The formality of the funeral ritual, where all concerned know what to do and what to expect, instantly disappears with the arrival of Richard, and Anne is denied the relative security and comfort which comes from her participation in a scenario that is known and familiar. Those who, together with her, were a part of that ritual, and had specific supporting roles to play (the fourteen men who accompany the corpse), are equally suddenly denied their roles, and their collective purpose is replaced by individual uncertainty about how to act. Instead of participants, they become observers. As such, their presence on stage during the action which follows reminds the audience in the theatre that collectively they have the physical power to intervene, but lack the necessary will to do so.

Richard now controls events through fear of what he might do, rather than through what he does, or even is realistically capable of doing. What happens to Lady Anne is shocking, yet understandable, *if* seen in imaginary performance by an active reader. It is akin to a nightmare in which a victim cries out for help, and though help is all around, it fails to materialise into action. Anne's seduction, or, as I prefer to think of it, her molestation by Richard, is witnessed by two equally helpless sets of spectators – on stage and off. Throughout the entire running time of this extraordinarily theatrical scene, only two lines are actually spoken by anyone other than Richard and Lady Anne, yet what they say, and its significance, can be understood only if recognition is given to the text being made by the silent, but far from inconsequential, characters on stage with them.

What I have suggested above in order to bring this scene to dramatic life will not please everyone. It is not, of course, *the* way to read what takes place, but it is *a* way of coming to terms with what to do with actors whom Shakespeare indicates are present, but does not clearly state why. My interpretation of this scene can quite easily be turned on its head. Let us suppose that the actress playing Lady Anne understands her character to be, not someone weak and vulnerable, but a calculating, mature woman who was never particularly close to her father-in-law, and who at this moment is merely fulfilling a public duty which cannot be avoided. Furthermore, that actress may see Anne as shallow and power-hungry, and suppose her initial response to Richard to be only a sham because she is secretly pleased and flattered by the close attentions of one so close to real political power. In such an interpretation, Anne cannot behave other than as she does *because the presence of the other on-stage characters monitoring her speech and actions* makes the occasion one in which it is necessary for her to present an appropriate public face. My point is that, in active reading, silent characters cannot and should not be ignored. If they are there then they are *making* a text, and the reader must consciously make interpretative decisions as to what to do with them.

Stage Properties

Many now distinguished actors have begun their careers as spear carriers in productions of classic plays in the English repertoire. It is lowly but dignified work, and, as we have seen, not without the potential for creating significance in an overall performance text. With or without his spear, the silent actor is always signifying something to an audience whenever he is on stage. Therefore the final aspect I want to examine in this essay, is not the actor, but his spear!

Stage properties are usually dismissed by the reader of plays as theatrical ephemera. However, they are almost always significant objects. The active reader needs to take note when a dramatist details the use of a specific prop, and then to decide imaginatively how it is to be employed in the action and why. Props help create mood and atmosphere; they can create locale, and they are an aid to actors in their creation of a role. The right choice of property can, as I will try to illustrate, actually impose, or at least reinforce, a specific interpretation of a scene.

In the printed text of the Richard/Lady Anne 'wooing' scene, two properties are mentioned: a ring given Anne by Richard, and a 'sharp pointed sword'. It is the latter that interests me. Towards the end of their verbal exchange, Richard apparently takes an extraordinary risk when he offers Anne

> ... this sharp pointed sword;
> Which if thou please to hide in this true breast,
> And let the soul forth that adoreth thee,
> I lay it naked to the deadly stroke,
> And humbly beg the death upon my knee.
>   (174–178)

He then proceeds to admit his guilt in the murder of Anne's father-in-law and husband. Why, then, does she not immediately kill him? In Olivier's film it was clearly supposed to be because she had already fallen under the irresistible charm and power of this superman. For Anne to seize the opportunity for revenge in the circumstance I have previously outlined (she is observed, young, vulnerable, isolated and a woman) is extremely hard, but perhaps not beyond the bounds of possibility. What might in fact (and does in my active reading) prevent her from attempting to kill Richard is the sword itself.

The only description of the weapon comes from Richard. Although the stage directions seem to indicate that it is a sword belonging to him ('he lays his breast open: she offers at it with his sword') there is nothing in the dialogue to suggest that it actually belongs to Richard. If the actor playing him were to move quickly and take a weapon from the hands of the silent on-stage characters (say from Tressel or Berkeley), then it could justifiably be a heavy, even a two-handed sword. Obviously there is a great deal of difference between offering a young and slight girl a dagger, and giving her a sword almost half as tall as herself. I have seen the former result in Anne's striking at Richard and being restrained by pinning her arm against the coffin. Encumbering her with a massive and unfamiliar weapon of war places her in a frustrating and humiliating posture, emphasising her helplessness in the hands of a supreme tactician like Richard.

The choice then, by the active reader, of what property to use when animating this scene, can show very different interpretations of the actions. If the reader decides the sword does belong to Richard, his personal weapon, light and, as he says, 'sharp', then the emphasis in the performance text will be on the magnitude both of the risks Richard takes and on his personal charisma in having the confidence and nerve required to take them. But, if the sword is heavy and cumbersome and belongs, not to Richard, but to one of the silent onlookers – a sword perhaps designed either for ceremonial use or for use by a professional soldier – Richard's providing

Anne with the weapon is shown as the action of a clever, calculating and totally cynical man.

This example, then, effectively demonstrates how a property can in itself be important in making meaning. A change in properties may radically alter interpretation, and make it possible to question the traditional audience response of reluctant admiration for Richard's virtuoso performance in seducing Anne. If an audience is made to see that there is no real physical risk involved for Richard, and that his 'victory' is hollow because the combatants were never remotely equal to begin with, then the view of the accomplished seducer must be more difficult to sustain.

To sum up: students should be made aware that nothing is ephemeral in a performance text. An individual sitting in an audience, or the active reader thinking at his or her desk, both encountering a play, are continually working at making a synthesis of the many and varied signals being transmitted by the characters, the words, the setting, the costumes, the gestures, lighting, properties, sound effects and so on. No single one of these signal generators (including printed dialogue) has dramatic priority over the rest. Active reading means being aware of the inter-connection of everything that is seen and heard in performance. It is therefore essential that students of dramatic literature (and not just *drama* students) are encouraged to take the imaginative risks that are a necessary and legitimate part of activating a printed text and making it live as a complete, if personal, performance.

The publishers are grateful to Penguin Books for permission to reproduce this article, the substance of which appears as part of Peter Reynolds' forthcoming book *Text into Performance* (February 1986). All quotations are taken from *The New Penguin Shakespeare*.

Examining Shakespeare

KEN WARREN

I

There are those who see the role of the examiner as a somewhat sinister one; to many he is a remote, anonymous figure, setting difficult tasks and pronouncing judgments that cannot be queried. There are others who see the entire examination process as an iniquitous activity, inherently harmful to the true appreciation of literature. To include a Shakespeare play in an examination is a kind of sacrilege; how can an understanding of drama be encouraged by the answering of questions on plot and character?

The examiner, of course, will not agree with any of these propositions or attitudes. He has a role as an assessor in a complex system of school and college examinations built up over many years but he also sees himself very clearly in an educational role; he gives direction to teaching, he sets targets to aim for, and in so doing acts as a stimulator of literary thought. His work complements the teaching process, helps to shape it and give it purpose; he is thus more an enabler than an inhibitor.

There can be no writer whose name appears more often in syllabus handbooks and on examination papers than Shakespeare's. This is the reflection of a universality of appeal matched by no other. This centrality is justified in terms of the intellectual and emotional depth of his plays; it is also justified in the extent of the appeal made to those who study his work. There is a long tradition of presenting and studying the plays, and this tradition manifests itself in the texts set for study in 16+ and A level examinations.

The examiner has several aims, all interdependent. He wants to find out how much a candidate knows about a chosen play; he wants to know whether or not a candidate can make a statement or pursue an argument about it; he wishes to know how far the candidate has involved himself with events and characters in the play. Such enquiry could be the subject of lengthy and interesting discussion, but in such a process there are too many variables and it is too time-consuming. The examiner seeks to effect communication mainly through the written word, and he aims to set a precise task so that those who undertake it have the opportunities to show their knowledge. There is no substitute for knowledge, and it follows that a candidate needs to have good, first-hand knowledge of the text. Reading the text of *Hamlet* or any other play is more useful – and rewarding – than reading a summary of the plot or any number of notes or character studies.

The second requirement is to be able to use this know-ledge to develop an argument or take part in a dialogue. There is a need to select ideas from the play to make a case or pursue a theme. Candidates may be asked to consider the motivation of character or to justify events. The third aspect, the quality of response that a candidate can bring to the play he has studied, is the most difficult part, but in fact the most indicative of full literary understanding.

In setting his tasks the examiner must take up main characters, incidents, motives and themes in the play under consideration. The question must not be too vast; 'Write all you know about Hamlet' is a badly drafted question – assuming that the candidate has read the play, where would he start? What is expected of him? On the other hand, to set a question asking for an analysis of the character and motives of the Porter in *Macbeth* would not be very profitable either – we know far too little about him from a single episode. It follows that the questions asked are intended to promote consideration of substantial issues; examiners like to concern themselves with main themes or important features of a play. Just occasionally, however, they are driven further into the corners of a play than they would wish; a text set for two examinations a year for four years requires 16 questions, and by convention they should not be repeated – finding this number of questions is sometimes difficult.

There is a qualitative difference between questions set for 16+ examinations and those set for A level. The 16+ question is more likely to depend on factual recall and the candidate will be expected to have a clear view of the sequence of events in a play, together with an understanding of why the characters behaved in the way they did. Questions are likely to be set on the action and on characterisation. 'Give an account of the events during the night preceding the Ides of March' or 'Consider the part played by Cassius' might be the bases of questions on *Julius Caesar*. It will be noted that the term 'bases' has been used – this is because these questions could also have 'tails': 'and how far Caesar's arrogance decided his fate' would be the continuation of the first question; 'showing how far you think Cassius had honest motives' of the second. These sub-questions require a judgment on the part of the candidate; he has already had the opportunity to display his knowledge of the text and his ability to select ideas from it. In assessing answers to such questions perhaps 15 marks would be allocated to the narrative element, 5 to the judgment; some candidates manage the straightforward account but damage their chances of gaining high marks by ignoring the sub-question or failing to come to terms with it. Specimen questions on *Twelfth Night* will illustrate the kinds of demands the examiner makes: 'Give an account of the gulling of Malvolio, and show how far you think this gulling is justified'; 'Examine the role of Maria in the play and identify those qualities that make her an attractive character to the audience.'

At A level the examiner makes the assumption – not always correctly, of course – that the main events of the play are known to the candidate. There are unlikely to be questions requiring purely narrative treatment, nor will there be questions answerable with straightforward character sketches. The candidate is expected to have knowledge, to be able to use it and to respond personally to the play, as before; nevertheless his increased intellectual capability will be tested by questions that require him to look more deeply into the play. If at 16+ he is expected to have a serial understanding of events from beginning to end, then at A level he is expected in addition to look in over the top of the play – to have an understanding of what Shakespeare is saying about fundamental human qualities, weaknesses and motives, and about the world in which man has his being. The questions asked will raise thematic issues central to the play. A question on *King Lear* might read: 'How far do you think the play asserts and denies the notion that "man is no more but such a poor, bare, forked animal"?' An answer would be expected to explore the deprivations to which man can be driven (Edgar and Lear himself come to mind), together with the goodness that survives evil and disaster (as in Cordelia and Edgar). It would also be possible to bring the Fool into the argument – his sanity is preserved throughout the hardships. The question clearly requires a sophisticated level of thought, as does the next: 'Consider Shakespeare's presentation of Cordelia and assess the dramatic significance of the part she takes in the tragedy.' This is not a straightforward character sketch – the candidate has to concern himself with Cordelia's provocative nature, her love and loyalty to Lear and the shocking inevitability of her death. The dramatic significances include the fact that the entire action is promoted by her refusal to express her love for her father in the terms he expected, her return with the King of France gives us false hope of resolution, and her death paves the way for the restoration of goodness. A characteristic question on *Antony and Cleopatra* might be: 'How is Shakespeare's portrayal of Cleopatra developed in her conversations and encounters with characters other than Antony?' – this requires keen perception and good powers of analysis! Other questions might be concerned with the structure of a play: 'The focus of *Antony and Cleopatra* shifts so constantly that, for all its power, the play gives an impression of confusion – discuss.' An answer would be expected to deal with the two aspects mentioned – power and confusion – in a study of the rapidity of changes of scene. On other occasions the interest might well be the dramatic qualities of a play; thus 'In *Macbeth* Shakespeare is not so much concerned with plausible characters as with theatrical and poetic effects – discuss' could promote an interesting essay.

It is evident that considerable literary experience is required for a good performance appropriate to 16+ and A level examinations. Knowledge of the text is vital at all stages, and this knowledge is expected to be such that a candidate can confidently and freely select incident and detail to support a case he is developing. Personal, informed response is valued at both levels, but is expected to have fuller expression at A; such response does not have to be directly expressed, of course; in many essays it is implicit in every line. As a very rough guide to his assessments the examiner at 16+ will allocate 8 marks to knowledge, 8 marks to arguing skills and 4 to informed personal response; at A level the marks will shift to 7 + 7 + 6. These patterns will be placed over any detailed marking scheme he may have and will help him to come to a final mark. The examiner of Shakespeare is really very fortunate; the text has its own delights, and almost all the answers he reads have some merits; he will warm to a lively piece of writing or respect the skills shown in a closely argued, well-illustrated essay. It is difficult to say anything new about a Shakespeare play but the responses of many candidates confirm the freshness of their approach and the liveliness of the teaching. In the best essays candidate and examiner enter into a dialogue – candidates are much less in awe of examiners than is sometimes thought; at all times the examiner is anxious to see that his questions have enabled candidates to write sensibly and sensitively about a play.

II

So far I have been concerned with answers in essay form. A long-standing feature of 16+ and A level examinations has been the context (or close-study) question where an extract from the play is printed and the candidate is referred to detailed questions on it. The requirements of the context (or close-study) question at 16+ are usually precise and limited. The following passage will serve as an example:

Macbeth. My dearest love.
          Duncan comes here tonight.
Lady M. And when goes hence?
Macbeth. Tomorrow as he purposes.
Lady M.   O, never
          Shall sun that morrow see!
          Your face, my thane, is as a book where men
          May read strange matters. To beguile the
              time,
          Look like the time; bear welcome in your eye,
          Your hand, your tongue: look like the
              innocent flower,
          But be the serpent under 't. He that's coming
          Must be provided for: and you shall put
          This night's great business into my dispatch;
          Which shall to all our nights and days to
              come
          Give solely sovereign sway and masterdom.

The detailed questions based on this extract might take the following form:

a) Who is coming, and what provision is to be made for him? (2 marks)
b) Explain: 'To beguile the time, Look like the time.' (2 marks)

c) What aspects of the characters of Macbeth and Lady Macbeth are brought out in this extract? (2 marks)

d) What does Lady Macbeth mean by 'solely sovereign sway and masterdom'? (2 marks)

e) Give two points from an earlier speech she makes that illustrate Lady Macbeth's intentions (2 marks).

The answers expected are these: (a) Duncan – he is to be murdered. (b) Macbeth should pass the time deceptively but apparently appropriately to his role as genial host. (c) Macbeth shows horror (or perhaps incomprehension) – his face the 'book where men may read strange matters'; Lady M. shows the keenest determination ('you shall put this night's great business into my dispatch'). (d) They alone will hold total power. (e) Any recognisable two references from the 'Unsex me here' speech.

It will be seen that the questions direct the candidates to the significant points made in (or implied in) the passage, and its relationship to the rest of the play. The questions are intended to be answered briefly, and the marks are awarded as the facts appear. There is a need for factual recall, but there is also some need for intelligent interpretation of the text. Examiners sometimes find themselves faced with lengthy answers that survey almost the whole of the play; facts should be given unadorned – as in answer (a) here – and there is not the slightest need for (or benefit in writing) paragraphs or even complete sentences where the answer can be provided in a very few words. Context exercises such as this one certainly test the candidate's knowledge of the play; they also allow him to earn marks quickly and to allocate the time saved to the essays.

At A level, questions based on extracts are more probing and less directed – the sequential element in the questioning illustrated above is often omitted. Thus candidates might be asked to study the following:

Cleopatra. Though age from folly could not give me
         freedom,
         It does from childishness. Can Fulvia die?
Antony. She's dead, my queen.

Look here, and at thy sovereign leisure read
The garboils she awak'd: at the last, best,
See when and where she died.

Cleopatra. O most false love!
Where be the sacred vials thou should'st fill
With sorrowful water? Now I see, I see,
In Fulvia's death how mine receiv'd shall be,

Antony. Quarrel no more, but be prepared to know
The purposes I bear; which are, or cease
As you shall give the advice. By the fire
That quickens Nilus' slime, I go from hence
Thy soldier, servant, making peace or war
As thou affects.

Cleopatra. Cut my lace, Charmian, come,
But let it be, I am quickly ill, and well,
So Antony loves.

Antony. My precious queen, forbear,
And give true evidence to his love, which stands
As honourable trial.

Cleopatra. So Fulvia told me.
I prithee turn aside and weep for her,
Then bid adieu to me, and say the tears
Belong to Egypt. Good now, play one scene
Of excellent dissembling, and let it look
Like perfect honour.

Antony. You'll heat my blood: no more.
Cleopatra. You can do better yet; but this is meetly.
Antony. Now, by my sword, –
Cleopatra. And target. Still he mends.
But this is not the best. Look, prithee, Charmian,
How this Herculean Roman does become
The carriage of his chafe.

Antony. I'll leave you lady.

The detailed questions might begin (a) by requiring the candidate to explain certain terms or phrases – here,

'The garboils', 'the sacred vials thou should'st fill with sorrowful water', 'quickens', 'as thou affects', 'play one scene of excellent dissembling', 'does become the carriage of his chafe'. An explanation of these will have a two-fold purpose: first there is the obvious testing one, while the second is to direct a candidate's attention to the difficulties in the passage to concentrate his mind on securing the fullest understanding. There might be six marks awarded for this part of the exercise. The main question, (b), will probably take the following form: 'What does this extract reveal of the relationship between Antony and Cleopatra and their attitude to each other?' This will be the more substantial section and 14 marks might be allocated.

The examiner will look for brief explanations of the words and phrases listed in (a). Thus, 'garboils she awakened' – the violent disorders she aroused; 'the sacred vials . . .' are the vessels filled with tears taken to Roman funerals (though there are other definitions); 'quickens' – brings life to; 'as thou affects' – as you choose: 'play one scene of excellent dissembling' – put on a skilful act of pretended feeling; 'does become the carriage of his chafe' – conveys his anger with appropriate manner. There are some possible variants here and marks would be awarded depending on the precision of explanation offered.

The second part, (b), requires close, careful, perceptive study of the passage given. While the perspectives of the rest of the play will never be far away from the candidate's mind, it is important that in his answer he does not range widely but concerns himself with the evidence he has in front of him. A short and compact essay is the kind of answer expected. Candidates will be expected to detect both the strength and the fragility of the relationship between Antony and Cleopatra, together with the conflicting motives of each. Antony might genuinely be moved by the death of Fulvia and he certainly feels he must take into account the political consequences of her actions. Cleopatra will not allow Antony to win: she teases him about his cold response to Fulvia's death, suggesting that this is how he will respond to hers. On

141

the other hand, were Antony more obviously moved Cleopatra would challenge him about the depth of his love for her, hence the references to acting and pretence, all of which provoke the rather serious Antony into further bluster and protestation. This encounter is an excellent demonstration of the confused emotions that exist throughout the play.

There is undoubted value in the close study of extracts such as these in establishing motive and character, and such interpretation and investigation might well form the basis of much good teaching at this level. It may be argued that 'the play's the thing' and that those studying the play should see it as a whole; this is certainly true, but the close reference to significant scenes or episodes helps to develop useful insights into a fully-informed global view.

III

Now for some points that candidates and teachers raise – these are in the main concerned with the essay answers that take up the larger part of the papers set. First: is there only one right answer to a question? The simple response is 'No'; examiners will accept – and accept cheerfully – what can be supported by evidence from the text. There are so many possible and legitimate variations of interpretation of character and motive that it would be scholastic folly to prescribe any one as the preferred statement. There are broad issues of agreement, of course, and it would be a brave candidate who thought Lear a wise man throughout the play, or who thought Brutus inspired by anything other than noble motives. However, within the broad areas of agreement there are many subtleties of interpretation. I have never held the elder Hamlet in very high regard, for example; if he slept every afternoon in his orchard he deserved what was coming to him. However, most people respect the late king highly!

Do we have to agree with the proposition stated in a question? If the question reads: 'Do you consider that

Henry V displays the most noble qualities of kingship?' do we have to agree that he does? The answer is 'No', provided that – and it is a very important proviso – a good case is presented for taking an opposite view. The examiner will enjoy reading a skilled presentation of a quirky case, but he must be convinced by it. While the examiner often offers a challenging question he is unlikely to mislead candidates by presenting an unusual point of view, so the best advice is to take the lead given; however, the candidate is asked for an expression of opinion, and this must appear in the answer. Questions of this kind are often introduced by the formula 'How far do you agree . . .' which is intended to be helpful.

Does the examiner ever set a trick question? The answer is 'No, not if he can help it!' The aim is to give candidates opportunities, not to set traps. It happens occasionally that some candidates do not see what the question is really about; that is unfortunate, but not really the fault of the examiner. A recent question asked: 'What important issues in the play are raised by Shakespeare's presentation of Othello as a Moor?' Many candidates ignored the phrase 'as a Moor' entirely; some of them did not appear to know that Othello was black – despite the many references. As a result there were many general essays on the character of Othello, in few of which were the central issues of racial attitude considered.

Do we have to quote? Answer: it is most advisable to do so, as an essay entirely devoid of quotation from the play tends to be bland, flat and rather dull. Much more important, however, is the fact that general points made gain much in substance if they are supported by textual reference. Falstaff may be described as a fat man, but the image gains greatly from the reference to the fact that he 'lards the lean earth as he walks along'. Mercutio is given to making explosive comments, but his impatience is vividly expressed in the line: 'The pox of such antic, lisping, affecting fantasticoes!' Kent's somewhat foolish provocation of Cornwall and his party is vividly conveyed in the lines:

Sir, 'tis my occupation to be plain:
I have seen better faces in my time
Than stands on any shoulder that I see
Before me at this instant.

The quotations from the text are best kept short and
apposite to the point being made. Examiners are not
greatly impressed by the appearance on a page of the
whole of the 'quality of mercy' speech, or the entire soliloquy beginning 'To be or not to be'. This is not because of
the familiarity of these speeches, but rarely can such
lengthy quotation be related to the argument being
developed except in the most general way. In fact
illustrative reference is best kept short and immediately
relevant. There is another matter to consider, and that
is accuracy of the quoted speeches. The examiner will
forgive a small slip in quotation except, of course, when
the omission of a 'not' makes nonsense of an argument;
however, extensive inaccuracy is more alarming, and the
candidate would have been better advised to 'refer'
rather than quote; if he cannot remember very much of
Lear's 'Blow, winds, and crack your cheeks' speech, he
can still usefully refer to 'drenched steeples' and 'all-
shaking thunder'. The inaccurate quotation is given
away by faulty punctuation, indicating that the writer
has not understood what he is quoting, and almost
immediately by broken-down metre. The loss of the
rhythms of Shakespeare's lines offends most examiners
very deeply indeed.

Another question: how important are the critics and
are we expected to refer to them? There is a formidable
range of critical apparatus so far as Shakespeare is
concerned. Possibly at 16+, certainly at A level, first-
hand reading of some critical works should be part of
the study. However, the views of the critics should be
used to develop the reader's own thinking about the play
he is studying. It follows that the examiner will not
necessarily be impressed by frequent references to
Bradley, Tillyard. Quiller-Couch or Wilson Knight. This
is not to denigrate these excellent scholars in any way,
but their function is to guide and inform, to open out

perspectives and give insights; the candidate, with the help of the critics, will – or should – come to his own, informed conclusions and these are what the examiner really wants to see. There are many study-aids about which are more or less helpful; many of them contain little more than a teacher and student can usefully build up themselves over a period of study. Whatever the merits of these aids, there is no substitute for first-hand knowledge of the text which allows the student to make his own assumptions and come to his own conclusions.

Next: is it a good thing to have seen a performance of the play? Yes, indeed it is – Shakespeare wrote for the stage and that is where his plays most obviously come to life. There is just one reservation – some productions take an unusual line and present their audiences with way-out interpretations of event or character. A critical discussion of the performance afterwards may well avoid the misapprehensions that some candidates betray in their written answers. If it is not possible to see a stage production teachers and students should not despair – there are films and videos; but Shakespeare comes to life in the imagination as completely as anywhere. It should be understood throughout the teaching process that we are always concerned with drama, with the give and take of lively dialogue, with conflict of character and with rapidly-moving events. It is not suggested that every reading of 'Once more unto the breach . . .' should be preceded by piling desks into a replica of the walls of Harfleur; however, the dramatic qualities of a text should be realised as fully as possible. We must emphasise the dramatic realism of the relationships in Shakespeare and the sheer impact of the words he uses. Some candidates in their writing refer to a novel or a poem; this may be just a slip, but it may also betray how they have perceived the play they have been considering.

IV

There are several other matters to be considered. For example: how important is expression; are errors of syntax and spelling taken into account? Perhaps curiously, there is no absolutely clear answer to this. The examiner in a literature paper will not allocate a specific mark for the quality of language used, but he will be influenced by it. The key is how well a candidate has communicated his ideas. The writer of clear, graceful prose has an obvious advantage over someone who cannot write a sentence that makes sense. Examiners will try very hard to interpret what they see before them, but it has to be said that, on occasion, the task is a hard one; sheets of convoluted writing with tortured sentence after tortured sentence eventually baffle the reader, however diligently he applies himself. It follows that good, clear expression gives the candidate a solid advantage, as it would in written work in any subject or activity.

Then there are some technical points. First, how long is a written answer intended to be? This really partly depends on how much a candidate can write in 45 minutes (or however long is allocated). Three sides of A4 paper is a very imprecise norm; but anything much shorter tends to arouse suspicion that the argument cannot have gone very deep; anything significantly longer suggests that the writer cannot marshal his points in concise form. An over-long answer has the additional disadvantage that it has taken up more than its share of time, thus constricting other opportunities. Some candidates and teachers ask: do we have to structure essays in note form? The only criterion here is that the notes should be useful to the candidate and not just a piece of 'window-dressing'. The examiner will not, in the ordinary way, read the notes; he is concerned with the short essays presented to him. If, however, a candidate has mis-timed his paper and all that appears for a final answer is in note form he will usually see what can be salvaged and award a mark accordingly. It should perhaps be emphasised that candidates should pace themselves through a paper; if four answers are asked for, then four answers should be written. There are assumptions that presenting three good answers and a fourth token offering is a good tactic; this is not so – a missing answer will take out the opportunity of earning, say, 20 marks and the 'good' answers have to be very good to compensate for this loss. Lastly in this section: what happens if the candidate answers more questions than are asked for? This is a rubric infringement and attitudes vary; most examining bodies ask examiners to mark everything and then allow what they can – the candidate is thus given maximum credit possible. In other cases, however, examiners are instructed to mark the first acceptable answers and delete the rest; this is a rather harsher view, and candidates are therefore warned!

There is another point relating to general practice in examinations, and that is the fact that no examiner works in isolation. In no case is his marking unsupervised or unchecked. There is a complex system of supervision organised by senior examiners and chief examiners; when the marking is over the candidate's work is presented for the award, itself a lengthy process based on statistical analysis and the judgments of the senior people. It is at this stage that special circumstances affecting candidates or centres are taken into account. Nothing that is written here suggests that anyone who has anything to do with the examining process maintains it is infallible; as in any other human activity mistakes are possible. However, there are usually ways and means of putting them right.

There are certain features of an examination script that sadden examiners, particularly at A level. First, there is the answer that is almost wholly narrative, with only the most distant bearing on the question set. Questions such as 'How far do you think Lear is responsible for his own downfall?' seem to have an uncanny knack of prompting long narrative accounts of the opening scene. Clearly, the knowledge is there but the candidate has not selected material relevant to the question; this is where the examiner writes: 'Too much narrative, too little analysis.' Then there is the question only half of which has been read: 'Consider the different kinds of jealousy displayed in *Othello*.' Many candidates tackling this listed, very fully, all the instances of jealousy that appeared in the play, but made no attempt to analyse the different kinds; they did not differentiate between sexual and professional jealousy, for example. Just occasionally the examiner is presented with an answer to the previous year's question; the mention of Petruchio might well be enough to trigger off an account of his taming of Katherina, but that was not the direction of the question on the current paper. Such answers have to be subject to a salvage operation when the examiner has to search for what is relevant in order to award a few marks. This also applies where a candidate has misread a question so that he writes on the wrong character or situation – a sad mistake which is somewhat disastrous.

It seems to me essential that candidates are made familiar with the layout of the papers they are to take before they enter the examination room. It is most helpful that a paper is immediately accessible to a candidate and that he should know where to look and what to expect. There is, however, little virtue in using previous papers as tests in their own right; they are rarely wholly applicable (with changes of set texts, for example) and the one thing a candidate knows for sure is that he will not see the same questions on the paper he actually sits. The whole psychology of the operation therefore seems to me to be wrong. Another essential preliminary is practice in devising and structuring answers. This can begin by knocking a question about in discussion, gradually shaping and refining the response; the answer can then be 'written up' without time limit at first, later in, say, 35 minutes. This process undoubtedly helps candidates develop their skills in selection, organisation and presentation of material.

Mention has already been made of the value placed on the individual response. Sometimes examiners are faced with thirty or so answers that cover exactly the same ground in an almost identical way. Credit is given to these answers on their merits – they represent diligence on the part of teacher and taught, but they are at best competent and often rather flat; in other words, they are not likely to qualify for the highest marks because their imaginative content is so small. This really reinforces the point that candidates should be encouraged to come to terms with the text and to develop their own responses to it. Candidates who are drilled through the text line by line cannot be said to have experienced the most lively teaching, and their attitude to Shakespeare might well be adversely coloured by the experience. There are lively and inventive methods, many of them the subject of other parts of this book; all the evidence shows that such lively teaching in fact enhances the pass rates – it certainly makes for more enjoyable study.

Examiners of Shakespeare, indeed of English Litera-ture as a whole, are aware that their dialogue with teachers and taught is somewhat one-sided. This need not be so; there are many channels through which obser-vations can be made and it is sometimes disappointing that so little use is made of them. Professional organis-ations collate teachers' comments on examination papers and these observations are considered by the appropriate committee within the examination boards. Individual letters are also given full consideration. Examiners write reports on each examination and these are usually published annually; in these, attempts are made to clarify issues and direct teachers' (and potential candi-dates') attention to approaches and techniques that will improve performances. These are designed to be forward-looking documents, not just post-mortems on the previous year's examination. They merit closer study than they sometimes seem to have had; points made by examiners, for example on how to deal with context or close-study questions, are not always taken up. Most examiners welcome opportunities to talk to teachers, in in-service courses, for example, and to share more closely in the professionl processes of teaching literature.

Lastly, much of this section has been concerned with the established practice of the formal external examin-ation, because that is the experience of the bulk of the candidates at the present time. However, the advent of the GCSE will undoubtedly spread more widely the variety of examination forms already available at CSE and O level GCE. While the externally set and examined paper will retain a place in the system, it seems likely that other methods of assessment will become increasingly popular. Course work and internally set and marked papers are already in use and the moderator of these has an advisory as well as an assessment role. There are examinations where candidates take their texts with them into the examination room; the Cambridge O level Plain Texts Literature examination is an obvious example.

There have been many developments in A level examining in recent years, among them the introduction of an internally set and marked, externally moderated paper and the substitution of a course-work file for one of the standard papers. 'Open text' examinations are also available. The AEB 660 scheme is particularly innovative as it offers two open-text papers and requires the submission of a file of course-work; this file comprises eight short essays and one longer piece based on texts of the centre's own choice subject to approval by the moderator appointed. There have been significant developments in Drama and Theatre Arts papers, all of which have Shakespeare as one of their main concerns. Cambridge and the AEB have schemes in this field. If a school has facilities for drama there are excellent opportunities for realising the text through performance. Teachers would be well advised to look around them at the opportunities presented by the different examination boards – they will perhaps be surprised by the extent to which new techniques of assessment have become established.

It should be remembered also that examiners are usually teachers, and many teachers are examiners. Teaching and examining are two aspects of one professional commitment – to ensure that the appreciation and enjoyment of literature are effectively encouraged. While Shakespeare cannot have envisaged the examination structure into which his plays have been fitted, he would surely have been pleased by the amount of appreciative attention his plays have attracted as a result. Had examiners existed in his time it is an interesting speculation as to what he would have said about them.

Teaching Shakespeare: A survey of recent useful publications

SUSAN MACKLIN

The actors are at hand; and, by their show,
You shall know all that you are like to know.
    (Peter Quince in *A Midsummer Night's Dream*, V.i)

Enlightened teaching of Shakespeare nowadays recognises the truth of Peter Quince's statement, Knowledge of a play is best acquired through imaginative or actual involvement in the three-dimensional, active world of the play. There has been considerable reform recently, some even describe it as a revolution, in methods of studying Shakespeare. Of course, academic study of a traditional kind is an integral part of the process, but on its own it cannot give students a complete understanding of the dramatic experience of the plays. Teachers are increasingly discovering new strategies for teaching Shakespeare, strategies which bring alive for their pupils the theatrical as well as the literary qualities of the plays.

'Texts are often read and studied as if they were long poems or most peculiar novels', writes John Russell Brown in the Introduction to his book, *Discovering Shakespeare: a New Guide to the Plays* (1981). 'Part of the revolution I seek is a change of priorities. Character analysis and the search for an underlying theme must wait until after the play has begun to come alive in a reader's imagination – with all the excitement and strength of theatrical performance, and with the sudden revelations and slow revaluations which are the ordinary signs of vitality in rehearsal.' This stimulating book, by a writer who is both a Professor of English and an experienced theatre practitioner provides an invigorating and detailed introduction to a new approach to the study of Shakespeare, an approach which is experimental, exploratory and open-ended.

It is the intention of this article to survey a selection of recent, useful publications relevant to the teaching of Shakespeare, with particular reference to some of those which focus on the dramatic experience of the plays. Many recent titles indicate this emphasis, for example *Shakespeare on Stage*; *Shakespeare in the Theatre*; *Playing Shakespeare*; *Teaching Shakespeare through Drama*; *'Othello': A Drama Approach to A Level English*. The approaches outlined vary, but what all the writers have in common is a concern for developing understanding of the dynamic nature of the dramatic experience.

English examiners are also very aware of the importance of the dramatic and theatrical, as well as the literary, qualities in the texts they set for study. Increasingly, it seems, they phrase the examination questions in such a way that they seem to expect knowledge and understanding not only of the literary quality of a play, but also – and importantly – of its theatrical nature. Candidates are asked to respond to questions such as what makes a Shakespeare play 'good theatre' or ensures its 'popularity on the stage'; they are invited to comment on such aspects of a play as its 'ritual action', 'comic relief', 'dramatic function', 'dramatic effect' or 'theatrical and spectacular elements'. Some questions even go so far as to invite candidates to respond to a play as if they were working on it in the theatre. Here is a recent example of the type:–

'There are as many different ways of directing *Macbeth* as there are directors. Each director has to make crucial decisions about what Shakespeare's play means and how the production will bring out the meaning.

What would you, as director, want to convey to the audience about *one* of the following three difficult problems:

    i) The witches

ii) Banquo's ghost
iii) The army scenes in Act 5?
and how would you do it?'
(Cambridge English Literature, Syllabus C, (Plain Texts) O.L., June 1984).

How are English teachers to prepare their pupils to deal successfully with questions such as this? Some teachers may even resent such questions, dealing as they do with dramatic concepts and theatrical conventions, and may be inclined to dismiss them as more appropriate to Drama or Theatre Arts than English Literature examinations. Other teachers will certainly find such questions challenging and exciting, but may feel that their training has not prepared them adequately to teach Shakespeare in this way. Fortunately, bookshops are full of recent publications providing stimulating reading on Shakespeare's plays in their theatrical context. Many of these are educational books or articles which suggest actual teaching strategies; others are works of more general interest.

For the purpose of this survey, I have divided the publications to be reviewed into three broad categories:–

1) Books and periodicals written specifically for teachers of English and Drama and their pupils. These I shall describe as Classroom Books, and this will be the longest section.

2) Books and articles of a more academic nature which, while relevant to the teaching of Shakespeare in secondary schools, are probably of use chiefly to teachers rather than their pupils, except for those working for A level. These I shall describe as Library Books.

3) The third category consists of books mainly about Shakespeare in performance. These are books written from a number of interestingly different points of view, by theatre practitioners such as directors, designers, actors and actresses and reviewers of stage and screen productions. These I shall describe as Theatre Books.

Section 1. Classroom Books

This section begins with brief reviews of two books which are best classified, perhaps, as reference or background books and it then goes on to consider a number of titles dealing with the teaching of Shakespeare in a wide variety of ways.

The Dramatic Experience: A Guide to the reading of plays, by J. L. Styan, and illustrated with drawings by David Gentleman, published first in 1965 and issued as a paperback in 1975 by CUP, is a book which is not solely about Shakespeare, but is nonetheless an extremely useful introduction to the reading of his plays. In his preface Professor Styan states that his aim is 'to make a contribution towards the stage-centred reform of drama teaching and appreciation. . . . reference in the text has been restricted to those plays most commonly met with in a study of English drama, especially those of Shakespeare'. The book combines theatre history with analysis of what makes a dramatic experience, considering such topics as the relation of stage and audience, the impact of the spoken word, the reality of dramatic character, plot and dramatic structure and the different kinds of drama such as comedy, tragedy, tragicomedy and problem play. It contains useful charts of theatrical history, reading lists and a glossary of theatrical terms. As an introduction to the vocabulary of drama and to Shakespeare's place in the development of the theatre, this is an excellent book.

Shakespeare and His Theatre, by John Russell Brown, also illustrated by David Gentleman, and published in 1982 by Penguin Books Limited, is a handsome book. It is lavishly and colourfully illustrated with drawings derived from contemporary sources and has a text by a distinguished Shakespeare scholar, which presents the fragmentary and sometimes contradictory evidence about Shakespeare's theatre in an exciting narrative style and which is also packed with detailed information: a stimulating and fascinating background book to Shakespeare studies.

Into Shakespeare: an introduction to Shakespeare

through drama, by Richard Adams and Gerard Gould, published in 1977 by Ward Lock Educational, is an extremely practical, classroom book. Each of its twelve chapters is concerned with one of Shakespeare's plays, and those selected are among those most frequently taught in schools. The book's approach is thematic and topics covered include the relationship between parents and children (*King Lear*); plots and conspiracies (*Julius Caesar*); authority (*Richard II*); war (*Henry VI Part 3*); quarrels (*Romeo and Juliet*) and discrimination (*The Merchant of Venice*). Each of the twelve units focuses on a key dramatic moment from one of the plays, examining its language as well as its action and – in doing so – offering opportunities for discussion, comprehension and writing as well as for spontaneous and polished improvisation, workshop presentations, school productions and project work. This is a very resourceful and imaginative book, of particular value, perhaps, to the English teacher keen to incorporate more practical drama work into the teaching of Shakespeare and looking for guidance on how to do so.

Teaching Shakespeare, by Veronica O'Brien, published in 1982 by Edward Arnold Limited, in the series 'Teaching Matters' is a short book of only five chapters and eighty-one pages. Despite its brevity, it is comprehensive in range, considering approaches to the teaching of Shakespeare throughout the secondary school from ways of introducing the plays at 11+ to methods of advanced level study. Throughout the book the teaching model recommended is that of the teacher as 'producer' and the classroom as a 'rehearsal room' where a company of actors are preparing a play as if for performance. This method is based on the premise that 'Pupils have, like any audience, the emotional and imaginative equipment to enter the world of the play and to enjoy the experience made possible by the fact that it is a play. It is in this enjoyment that understanding begins'. This is an extremely practical handbook, encouraging teachers and pupils to read the texts in a spirit of discovery and enquiry and suggesting a variety of teaching strategies, useful to both experienced and new teachers of English. It also contains a helpful, short bibliography.

Shakespeare on Stage by David A. Male is a series first published in 1984 by CUP and intended for students of Shakespeare taking literature, drama or theatre arts courses in schools and colleges. Each book in the series looks at a particular play in performance, concentrating on the play as dramatic art rather than simply as a text on a page. Three titles have so far been published, *Macbeth*, *The Winter's Tale* and *Antony and Cleopatra*. In size and format each slim volume resembles a Royal Shakespeare Company programme – a deliberate resemblance – and each contains a number of photographs of recent and contrasting productions of the play by the Royal Shakespeare Company. The volume on *The Winter's Tale*, for example, compares the 1969 production of the play, directed by Trevor Nunn and designed by Christopher Morley, with two later productions, those of 1976 and 1981. Students are encouraged to consider each play in the light of the different productions and to become aware of the varying ways in which directors and designers have approached the play and its governing ideas and found different solutions to the challenge of presenting it on stage. The particular concern of these books is the relationship between the ideas and images in the texts and the ways in which these are visually realised on stage in performance. Each book concludes with suggestions for individual and group practical and written work. This series, studying Shakespeare's plays from the point of view of professional directors especially, would provide ideal course books for pupils preparing for examinations in which they might expect to be asked questions such as the one quoted at the beginning of this article. The volume on *Macbeth* describes three different approaches to the play and what the examination question refers to as the 'problem' of the witches is discussed and illustrated in particular detail.

Text and Performance is another valuable recent series designed to help students achieve a fuller recognition of the equal importance of both literary analysis and theatrical experience in their study of plays. The series is published by Macmillan and the General Editor is Michael Scott. Each compact volume follows the same basic pattern. Part One provides a critical introduction to the play, using the techniques and criteria of the literary critic in examining the manner in which the work operates through language, imagery and action. Part Two takes the enquiry further into the play's theatricality by focusing on selected productions of recent times so as to illustrate points of contrast and comparison in the interpretation of different directors and actors, and to demonstrate how the drama has worked on the modern stage and, often, on film. Each volume includes a single–page plot synopsis and information about sources at the beginning and a very helpful, carefully selected Reading List at the end. Photographs of recent stage, and occasionally film, productions of the play are contained in Part Two. The series was first published in 1983 and the list, now in 1985, includes nine of Shakespeare's major plays, as well as Marlowe's *Doctor Faustus* and Jonson's *Volpone*. Further Shakespeare titles are in preparation. This is a most lively and informative series, probably most useful to students studying for Advanced Level Examinations.

The Group Approach to Shakespeare, by David Adland, published by Longman in the early 1970s, is a series aimed at younger pupils, useful to those preparing for O Level or CSE examinations or the new 16+ or GCSE. The series contains separate volumes on *Romeo and Juliet*; *The Merchant of Venice*; *Twelfth Night* and *A Midsummer Night's Dream* and the emphasis is on practical work on the plays. Each book provides lists of suggestions for ways of working on every scene in the play including activities such as conversations between groups of characters, interviews and stage design projects for pairs and larger groups of children.

The Poet's Method, from a series entitled *In Shakespeare's Playhouse*, was published by David and Charles in 1974, and written by Ronald Watkins and Jeremy Lemmon. The purpose of the series is to investigate in detail the nature of Shakespeare's craftsmanship. *The*

Poet's Method describes the kind of playhouse in which Shakespeare worked and argues that it favoured the growth of a dramatic method fundamentally different from the theatrical practice of our own times. The principles of investigation suggested in this book are put into practice in subsequent volumes which analyse individual plays as if in performance 'in Shakespeare's playhouse'. *The Poet's Method* thus provides an approach which is different from that of some of the more recently published studies concentrating on Shakespearean productions in the modern theatre. It is a useful book for students embarking on practical criticism of Shakespeare's language, as one of its central concerns is with the nature of poetic drama, seen in the context of the physical theatre for which it was written.

English through Drama: a way of teaching, by Christopher Parry, published by CUP in 1972, is a book by a teacher whose approach is also greatly influenced by a consideration of the conditions in Shakespeare's playhouse. The book describes the present–day development of the pioneering work in English teaching by Caldwell Cook at the Perse Boys School in Cambridge during the early years of this century. There are frequent references to the specialist English teaching room at the Perse, known as the Mummery, with its facilities for simple stage lighting, music and simple costume. The Mummery has in its design many of the features of an Elizabethan playhouse – it is on an intimate scale which brings audience and performers close together, and it is a space which, by its nature, puts great reliance on the imagination's power of response to the spoken word. Chapter Six is devoted to the teaching of Shakespeare and gives a vivid account of the strategy whereby boys from the age of about twelve study Shakespeare through classroom performances. Later chapters deal with some less verbal approaches such as *Macbeth* as dance-drama and *Hamlet* in mime.

Scripted Drama: A practical guide to teaching techniques, by Alan England, published by CUP in 1981, is another account of a particular methodology: this time that of a drama specialist. It is written out of the conviction that, as plays are by their nature intended for performance, active approaches to them will always be most educationally profitable. This is a stimulating book for teachers of both English and Drama. Although it is not exclusively concerned with the teaching of Shakespeare, it contains many references to his plays, illustrating and justifying a variety of practical approaches to them.

This section concludes with brief mention of some educational journals which regularly publish articles and reviews of interest to the teacher of Shakespeare. English teachers will already be familiar with periodicals such as *English in Education, The English Magazine* and *The School Librarian* all of which frequently contain reviews of new books, and articles on teaching strategies, relevant to the study of Shakespeare. *The English Magazine* is a national, termly magazine for secondary English teachers, published by the ILEA English Centre. The Centre provides in-service support for secondary English teachers within the ILEA and it also produces teaching materials as well as the termly magazine. Recently, a series of most useful booklets has been devised by teachers on courses at the Centre, on a number of English set texts, including *Romeo and Juliet* and *Macbeth*, intended for use with classes tackling the plays for CSE.

There are also several periodicals published mainly by and for teachers of Drama. Two of the most useful of these are *London Drama Magazine* and *2D* (Dance and Drama magazine); both of them have recently carried articles of special relevance to the teaching of Shakespeare. *London Drama*, Volume 6, Number 8, Summer 1983, was devoted almost entirely to the subject, with contributions from teachers, actors and directors describing and discussing a number of different schemes all devised to assist teachers and pupils in their study of Shakespeare's plays. On one A4 page Dorothy Heathcote offers teachers of *Hamlet* twelve different ideas for drama activities designed to further understanding of the play. These twelve ideas may be developed in a dozen other directions, prompting ideas for similar strategies for work on other plays; an excellent and very succinct article. *2D*, Volume 3, Number 3, Summer 1984, has among its contents two useful articles. One, 'Some Experiences with Shakespeare', is an account by an advisory teacher, Simon Taylor, of workshop sessions he has led on aspects of Shakespeare; the other, '*Othello*: A Drama Approach to A Level English', is jointly written by two English teachers describing the ways in which they are developing their own approach to the Cambridge Mode III Alternative A Level English syllabus. In the next issue *2D*, Volume 4, Number 1, Autumn 1984, an article, entitled 'Not so Bard after all' by head of English Paul Bailey, deals most interestingly with approaches to the teaching of Shakespeare in an 11 – 14 middle school.

Finally in this section, mention should perhaps be made of the latest technological innovations. Computer programmes, aimed at students of Shakespeare, have been produced by both Penguin and Oxford Digital Enterprises. Penguin Study Software is intended particularly for examinees and, as the programmes are literary in emphasis and technically easy to operate, they would be useful for reference or revision work by individual senior pupils. Oxford Digital Enterprises, on the other hand, have produced four adventure games, interspersed with question and answer sessions, complete with sound and pictures, inspired by *Macbeth*. This project was given qualified approval in a recent *Times Literary Supplement* review, anticipating the likely popularity of such study aids:– 'Notoriously unlucky, *Macbeth* has the doubtful honour of being the first Shakespeare play to be turned into a computer game; the pursuit of goblins through Athenian Woods and ghosts over Elsinore's battlements must soon follow'. Perhaps a useful addition to the more familiar methods of study?

Section 2. Library Books

This section is concerned with the more scholarly approach to Shakespeare studies and the field here is so vast that the selection of a few especially helpful titles has been very difficult. All teachers will have their favourite literary critics and, inevitably, many valuable works of recent scholarship have been left out of this list. What is offered in the paragraphs below is a limited and personal selection of titles which, in my view, deserve inclusion in the school library where they will provide interesting reading for teachers and their A level students. Many of the books mentioned are likely to be already on the shelves, but they seemed to me worthy of repeated recommendation. There is, once again, a bias in the selection in favour of books dealing as much with Shakespeare's theatrical as with his literary skill. The first in the list is, in fact, a classic work which has recently been reissued in a new, enlarged paperback edition. The following titles are all of newer vintage.

Shakespeare's Stage, by A. M. Nagler, Yale University Press, was originally published in 1917 and has recently been reissued in paperback, enlarged and with an up–to–date bibliography. The book is illustrated with three of the most famous illustrations available to the student of Shakespeare's stage – the Swan Theatre, London, sketched by Johannes de Witt; the detail from the frontispiece to 'Roxana Tragaedia' and the detail from the frontispiece to 'The Tragedy of Messalina'. It also contains extracts from a number of interesting original documents. Episodes from Shakespeare's plays are examined in detail in the light of the documentary evidence. This is not a beginner's book. Some previous knowledge of the major plays is essential to follow the always illuminating debate. Take, for example, the following short paragraph in which four of Shakespeare's plays and a play by two contemporary dramatists are mentioned within a very short space:–

'For the orchard and graveyard scenes in *Romeo and Juliet* we have assumed that trees were placed on stage. Such three-dimensional trees were also used, no doubt, in *As You Like It*: Orlando needed a tree on which to fasten his love poem, and he speaks of other trees on which he means to carve Rosalind's name. Chambers once suggested that such trees appear through the trap.

I regard this as unlikely; in all probability the traps were used only for magical effects. The bower for the play within the play in *Hamlet*, which Chambers has rising out of the trap, was carried in by stagehands, and the same is true of the bower in *Much Ado About Nothing*. But when a bower was conjured up by magic, it did spring out of the trap. This was the case in *A Looking Glass for London and England*, by Robert Greene and Thomas Lodge, where the ground is smitten with magic wands and a magnificent bower rises up out of the main trap.' (*Shakespeare's Stage* p. 62–63.)

In addition to mention of four of Shakespeare's plays, there is also reference in this paragraph to the fascinating subject of how the traps in the stage may have been used, and to Chambers and the scholarly controversy his work engendered. Nagler's book, compact in size yet full of detailed information, provides excellent material for sixth-form study. It is prefaced with a challenge to the student to take the study of the stage history of Shakespeare's plays seriously:–

'This book is a study of the theatre with which Shakespeare the dramatist had to work. He lived in an age when the closest harmony prevailed between literature and the theatre. The student of Elizabethan drama cannot ignore the stage. If he is unwilling to concern himself with the workings of the theatre, he will do well to take up Shakespeare's sonnets rather than his plays.' (*Shakespeare's Stage* p. xi.)

Shakespeare Our Contemporary, by Jan Kott, first published in 1965, and issued as a University Paperback in 1967, is a book which has exercised considerable influence on the teaching of Shakespeare during the last twenty years. Kott, a Pole who has suffered both the Nazi terror and the Stalinist repression, interprets Shakespeare in the light of his personal experience of twentieth-century tumult and danger. Peter Brook, in his Preface to the book, writes:–

'Shakespeare is a contemporary of Kott, Kott is a contemporary of Shakespeare – he talks about him simply, first-hand, and his book has the freshness of the writing by an eye-witness at the Globe or the immediacy of a page of criticism of a current film. To the world of scholarship this is a valuable contribution – to the world of theatre an invaluable one.' This is a stimulating, often provocative, book to put into the hands of sixth-formers.

John Russell Brown's recent book, *Discovering Shakespeare*, has already been recommended. In addition to this, many of his earlier books and articles deserve space in the school library, especially, perhaps, *Shakespeare's Plays in Performance* (1966) and *Free Shakespeare* (1974). The latter encourages new ways of looking at the plays, arguing that Shakespeare both in performance and in academic study needs to be freed from sometimes limiting, traditional treatment, and suggesting many practical ways in which this freeing can be achieved.

A scholarly and historical book, of great interest to teachers and senior pupils, is J. L. Styan's *The Shakespeare Revolution: Criticism and Performance in the Twentieth Century*, published by CUP in 1977. In it, Professor Styan charts the changing practice of staging Shakespeare, from the 'dramatic cathedral' productions of the later Victorians and the early experiments of William Poel and Granville Barker to the empty-space, in-the-round, non-illusory statements of, among others, Tyrone Guthrie, Peter Brook and Peter Hall, which have accentuated the imaginative, visionary quality of Shakespeare's work. Professor Styan also assesses the influence of the theories of such major scholars as Bradley, Bradbrook, Wilson Knight and Leavis and he demonstrates how, as academics and critics have begun to see with playhouse eyes, the relationship between study and stage has grown ever closer. The book is generously illustrated with an excellent selection of drawings and photographs.

Dr. Ralph Berry has recently published a number of books all making major contributions to contemporary Shakespeare studies. These would all be of great value to the school library:– *On Directing Shakespeare – Interviews with Contemporary Directors* (1977) Croom Helm; *The Shakespearean Metaphor: Studies in Language and Form* (1978) Macmillan; *Changing Styles in Shakespeare*

(1981) Allen and Unwin, and *Shakespeare and the Awareness of the Audience* (1985) Macmillan.

In *Shakespeare in the Theatre*, by Richard David, published by CUP in 1978, Shakespeare's plays are discussed in relation to major English productions of them during the seventies. The author considers in detail moments in actual performance that have seemed to him successful and also moments that have seemed to impair the dramatic effects intended by Shakespeare; he raises many questions and draws some interesting conclusions about the nature of Shakespeare's art in particular and about the art of the theatre in general. This book, which is very clearly written and illustrated throughout by excellent black and white photographs of the productions being discussed, is one to provoke lively sixth-form discussion and debate.

It seems to me admirable that there is now such a wealth of visual material relating to the study of Shakespeare. Students need a great deal of help in learning to appreciate the spectacular and theatrical aspects of the plays, and in coming to understand them as a visual, as well as a literary, art form. The availability in so many books and periodicals of good–quality production photographs, reproductions of paintings and original sketches and drawings provides excellent teaching material and gives students a real chance to develop imaginative and visual concepts of Shakespeare on the stage as well as on the page. This is, perhaps, especially important in these days of tight budgets and high prices when schools often find theatre visits a financial impossibility. Two especially helpful books offering predominantly pictorial information are *Shakespeare on the Stage: An illustrated history of Shakespearian Performance* (1973) Collins, written by Robert Speaight and lavishly illustrated with almost two hundred black and white pictures as well as thirty-two pages of full colour plates; and *A Pictorial Companion to Shakespeare's Plays* (1982) Muller, devised and designed by Robert Tanitch. This book, by a teacher who is head of English in a comprehensive school, brings together in words and superb black and white illustrations some of the most famous characters, scenes and speeches in Shakespeare's plays; there is no commentary, Shakespeare's words and the accompanying pictures speak eloquently for themselves – a bold and exciting book.

Shakespeare: An Illustrated Dictionary (1978) OUP, by Stanley Wells, contains more than 150 photographs and drawings, and is an attractive and informative reference book for students and teachers. Also useful is Stanley Wells's *Shakespeare: The Writer and His Work* (1978) Longman, a concise survey linking Shakespeare's work with his life and background.

Two books by Judith Cook deserve strong recommendation. It is perhaps noteworthy that, until quite recently, Shakespearean commentary has remained a largely male province. *Women in Shakespeare* (1980) Harrap, is a study of the whole range of Shakespeare's female roles, accompanied by comments from actresses who have played the parts revealing the fascinating insights they have gained into Shakespeare's characterisation. Judith Cook has followed this book with another, *Shakespeare's Players* (1983) Harrap, in which she develops her theme, looking at the whole range of Shakespeare's major roles and those who have played them. Both books are illustrated.

Shakespeare the Director (1982) B and N Imports, by Ann Pasternak Slater, is another recent book also focusing on the theatrical qualities of Shakespearean drama; it has chapters on the following topics and their importance to a proper understanding of the plays:– silence and pause; kissing and embracing; weeping; costume and properties.

This section ends with an acknowledgement of the continuing value to teachers and senior pupils of periodicals, the annual publication *Shakespeare Survey* (Cambridge) and the American *Shakespeare Quarterly* (Washington D.C.), both offering the means of keeping abreast of Shakespeare studies.

Section 3. Theatre Books

Space does not allow this section to be other than very brief. It is, nonetheless, in my view, a very important section. In it, I have put together a list of books by writers who are all, in one way or another, involved in the practicalities of Shakespeare in performance. The creative insights of these writers make stimulating reading and suggest many ideas which may be adapted into imaginative teaching strategies. Some of these books will certainly be of interest to those whose teaching includes production, either of scenes in the classroom or of full-scale school productions of Shakespeare.

At the head of the list is a book which, although not very recent, has been to me and many others a continual source of inspiration since its publication in 1968: this is, of course, *The Empty Space* by Peter Brook (Penguin). It is a work of wisdom and vision by one of our greatest directors and, although not specifically concerned with Shakespeare, it is so illuminating an account of a director's understanding of the theatre, of his approach to texts, to actors and to the whole process of rehearsal and production, that I have always found it to be rich in ideas for teaching. I have, for example, often adapted and used with sixth-formers the exercise (described on pages 120–122 of the 1969 hardback edition) in which the director is exploring with his actors the many different levels of meaning and changes of style within a short scene from *Romeo and Juliet*.

Two books by Grigori Kozintsev, the great Russian theatre and film director, also make fascinating reading. *Shakespeare: Time and Conscience*, first published in Great Britain in 1967, includes a provocative essay about the production and staging problems presented by Shakespeare's plays, a masterful analysis of *King Lear* and a long, penetrating essay on *Hamlet*. This was followed in 1977 by *King Lear: The Space of Tragedy*, a diary of Kozintsev's experience in making his film of the play.

Another book describing, in the form of a diary, the

166

process of theatrical creation, is David Selbourne's *The Making of 'A Midsummer Night's Dream': An Eye-Witness Account of Peter Brook's Production from First Rehearsal to First Night.* This book, published by Methuen in 1982, more than a decade after the production it describes, is both a detailed account of one of the most remarkable Shakespearean productions of the century, and a critical reflection on the process of theatrical creation.

Playing Shakespeare, by John Barton (1984) Methuen, is a book which evolved from a television series screened on Channel 4 in 1984, in which RSC director John Barton and a group of well-known Shakespearean actors gave 'master-classes' on playing Shakespeare. Much of the book is in the form of a dialogue between Barton and the actors, conversations in which they discuss such important topics as The Two Traditions – Elizabethan and Modern Acting; Language and Character – Making the Words One's Own; Irony and Ambiguity – Text that isn't what it seems; and many more. This is an admirable and most educational book, revealing the detailed hard work and professionalism of actors engaged in the interpretation of Shakespeare for a modern audience. Also from the actors' point of view is a new book, *Players of Shakespeare: Essays in Shakespearean Performance by Twelve Players with the Royal Shakespeare Company*, edited by Philip Brockbank and published in 1985 by CUP. This is a unique account, by twelve distinguished actors, of the preparation and performance of a Shakespeare role each has played in a production with the Royal Shakespeare Company.

Other useful books, though more concerned with Shakespeare's plays from the perspective of the audience than the actors, are:- *The Living World of Shakespeare: A Playgoer's Guide* by John Wain, first published in 1964, reissued with a new preface in 1978 by Macmillan; *Going to Shakespeare* (1978) Allen and Unwin, by J. C. Trewin, a drama critic who draws on his experience of having seen over 1,500 performances of Shakespeare; and *Shakespeare in Perspective* (1982) Allen and Unwin, two paperback volumes of essays from the radio and television commentaries on the BBC TV Shakespeare, introducing television audiences to the plays from the points of view of distinguished actors and actresses and well-known writers and broadcasters.

Confessions of a Counterfeit Critic: A London Theatre Notebook 1958–71 by Charles Marowitz, published in 1973, and *A View of the English Stage 1944–1965* by Kenneth Tynan, published in 1975 by Davis-Poynter, are both books by theatre critics who have played leading roles in the development of drama and theatre in the mid-twentieth century and their reviews of Shakespearean and other productions make always stimulating and sometimes provocative reading.

Finally, mention of two theatre periodicals which frequently contain excellent material for use in the teaching of Shakespeare. *Plays and Players* is a well-known, readily available, monthly magazine reviewing current productions in London, the regions and abroad and carrying articles on a range of theatre topics. The May 1985 issue, for example, included an interview with Juliet Stevenson, the actress playing Rosalind in the newly-opened production of *As You Like It* at Stratford; she discussed her interpretation of the role ('I think the play has something to say about Greenham Common – I really do') and the modern–dress, surrealistic design of the production: an article, accompanied by a full-page photograph of Rosalind and Orlando on set, their images reflected in a stage lake, which might well provoke some lively classroom discussion.

New Theatre Quarterly has been described as a vital forum for theatre studies and it offers theatre news, analysis and debate in a scholarly and informed manner. Its editors are Clive Barker and Simon Trussler and it is a successor journal to the old *Theatre Quarterly* (1971–1981). The first issue of the relaunched journal appeared in February 1985 and contains at least three articles of interest to teachers and students of Shakespeare. Back numbers of the original *Theatre Quarterly* are also available and contain much invaluable material such as, for example, *Staging Macbeth – Productions Past and Present* in Vol. 1, No. 3, 1971 and *Craig and*

Stanislavsky Collaborate on Hamlet at the Moscow Art Theatre in Vol. 6, No. 22, 1976 – a fascinating and fully documented account of a now legendary production.

Postscript

In connection with their major productions of plays by Shakespeare and other dramatists whose works are likely to be school set texts, many theatres nowadays publish excellent resource or background packs for schools. These normally contain not only information about the production and the play, but also suggestions for follow-up work of various kinds. The National Theatre, The Young Vic and the St George's Theatre, Islington, are among those which have recently produced very useful teaching materials on some of Shakespeare's plays.

Shakespeare Video Workshops by David Whitworth are another, much more expensive, example of performance-centred resource material. *The Comic Spirit* and *The Tortured Mind* are two new videos (1983) exploring themes in Shakespeare's comedies and tragedies. They have been specially prepared for O and A level students and the material on the tapes is based on the New Shakespeare Company Workshops at the Roundhouse, adapted and extended for ILEA television. These videos will serve as a complement to textual analysis, enriching and broadening students' views of the four plays on each tape by looking at crucial scenes in each, exploring the psychology of the characters and the impact of performance. Each video is available in either VHS or Betamax format.

Knowing Hawks from Handsaws

LINDA COOKSON

A practical survey of the following series of
Shakespeare editions:
The Arden Shakespeare (Methuen)
The Kennet Shakespeare (Arnold)
The Macmillan Shakespeare (Macmillan)
The New Cambridge Shakespeare (Cambridge
  University Press)
The New Penguin Shakespeare (Penguin)
The New Swan Shakespeare (Longman)
The New Swan Shakespeare, Advanced Series
  (Longman)
The Oxford Shakespeare (Oxford University Press)

Editions compared

The aim of this article is to compare and act as a guide
to some of the many single-text editions of Shakespeare's
plays which are currently available in paperback and
which fall within the price range of c. £1.10 – c. £3.50.
It will examine in detail the contrasts in presentation
and content which distinguish the different series, and
a short conclusion will offer the writer's own views about
the appropriateness of particular editions in relation to
specific teaching aims and needs.

Presentation

I'll begin with the COVERS, since these do, after all, influence the expectations that a potential reader will form about the attractiveness (or otherwise) of the play in question. Something dull and dog-eared is hardly likely, after all, to generate much enthusiasm or excitement. Still more significantly, covers can also play quite a formative role in shaping the initial assumptions with which a new reader will then approach the text itself. They can, for example, establish an immediate focus on the play as a theatrical performance and thus encourage in the reader a continued readiness to identify page with stage. Alternatively, they can act as a kind of graphic shorthand, whereby a particular image is used to suggest to the reader the mood or idea that will then dominate the play. Both of these considerations have clearly played a part in dictating the cover designs of all eight of the series in this survey – albeit to rather varying effects.

Colour, naturally enough, has become an important weapon in the fight to catch the eye and the interest. All of these series use colour in their covers – although with widely differing degrees of subtlety. At one end of the tonal range Longman launches a full-frontal assault on the eyeball with a head and shoulders of Shakespeare (looking decidedly queasy) in fluorescent blue (*New Swan Shakespeare, Advanced Series: Othello*); at the more restrained end, *The New Cambridge Shakespeare* offers a discreet background of Wedgewood blue ('Looks like toilet paper,' said one of my pupils discouragingly). Like *The New Cambridge Shakespeare*, *The Macmillan Shakespeare*, *The Oxford Shakespeare* and *The New Penguin Shakespeare* all opt for a uniform background colour. In the first two cases, the chosen colour is black – producing an effect that is both striking and sophisticated (although *The Oxford Shakespeare* then gilds the lily, by blazoning the series title in lavish gold lettering); *The New Penguin Shakespeare*, on the other hand, goes for white – again, simple and attractive, but producing a slightly more cluttered appearance than plain black. *The Kennet Shakespeare* and *The Arden Shakespeare* change the background colour from volume to volume. The effect is less than satisfactory in the case of *The Kennet Shakespeare*: in the absence of a high-gloss finish, the colours become flat and drab. *The Arden Shakespeare*, however, becomes a veritable triumph in technicolour: pupils seem almost unanimous in applauding the richness and vibrancy of its covers.

Designs vary considerably from series to series. *The New Cambridge Shakespeare* – in keeping with its declared aim to be 'more attentive than some earlier editions have been to the realisation of the plays on the stage' – concentrates on the plays in performance. Its covers are intricate line drawings depicting a sixteenth century production of each play. Interestingly, only actors and scenery change – the stage and audience remain the same from volume to volume (in itself an intriguing idea, although the failure of the watching faces to register any emotional difference between Petruchio's mealtime tantrums and Romeo's discovery of his dead wife's body becomes a little sinister). *The Kennet Shakespeare* and *The Macmillan Shakespeare* are similarly committed to representing the plays in the theatre. *The Kennet Shakespeare*, like *The New Cambridge Shakespeare*, offers line drawings, but here the outcome is decidedly less happy: results vary from the trite to the embarrassing to the frankly perplexing (try writing a caption to the front of *Macbeth* or *As You Like It*!). *The Macmillan Shakespeare* – perhaps wisely, in the light of the weaknesses of the *Kennet* covers – neatly sidesteps the problems facing an illustrator. Its covers incorporate beautifully produced colour photographs from recent productions (*Othello*, for example, gives us Paul Schofield's 1980 interpretation of the title role).

The cover designs of the remaining series reject the theatrical in favour of the emblematic. *The New Penguin Shakespeare* edition of *Julius Caesar*, for example, depicts a laurel wreath and a bloody dagger (not the last word in originality perhaps, but highly preferable, it seems to me, to their *Romeo and Juliet*, which shows a skull impaled on a lute against a background of crossed swords). *The New Swan Shakespeare* edition of *Julius*

Caesar – unobjectionably, but rather predictably – carries a drawing of a bust of Caesar. And *The Oxford Shakespeare* edition of the same play, in line with the series format, sets a small, brightly-coloured painting (in this case, of Caesar himself) like a badge against the black background. The joker in the pack, as far as *Julius Caesar* editions go, proves to be *The Arden Shakespeare* – where the combination of full moon, clouds, Caesarian bust, gaunt tree, autographed picture of Caesar, Salvador Dali hills, and unidentified box reminds me of nothing so much as of a Benson and Hedges advert. In fairness, however, this venture into the surreal is not characteristic of the series as a whole. Its cover designs, paintings commissioned from the Brotherhood of Rural- ists, have in general an attractive simplicity that evokes a powerful sense of continuity with the past.

To move on from covers, LAYOUT, of course, is a further aspect of presentation that has a significant influence on the way in which a new reader reacts to an edition. Clarity of typeface, pagination, lineation, the accessi- bility and legibility of explanatory notes – all are factors which can have a direct bearing on the total reading experience.

Happily, all eight of these editions carry a text that is admirably clearly printed. All but *The Arden Shake- speare* (which uses abbreviations and italics) assist the unfamiliar reader by giving the full name of each speaker in capital letters before every new speech (although *The New Swan Shakespeare* disrupts rather than aids the textual flow by the curious practice of printing the characters' names *above* the words spoken). Moreover, all of the editions number the lines of the text (*The Oxford Shakespeare, The Macmillan Shakespeare* and *The New Penguin Shakespeare* number every tenth line; the others number every fifth). As a minor point, however, since this process can lead to unnecessary confusion with page numbers, it would be helpful if all editions followed the format of *The Oxford Shakespeare, The New Penguin Shakespeare* and *The New Swan Shakespeare* and set page numbers at the foot of the page, in the centre of the line. Only *The New Penguin*

Shakespeare is a little unclear in its Act and Scene divisions (by affording very little space to scene changes and by the non-standard use of the right-hand side of odd-numbered pages for this purpose), and all editions are generally sound and helpful in their use of running heads at the tops of pages (although these are inexplicably absent from the *Macmillan* edition of *Twelfth Night*). *The Arden Shakespeare* could, perhaps, be improved in this respect, if it were to follow the more usual method of placing Act and Scene references at the head of each separate page, rather than dividing the information over two pages; *The New Cambridge Shakespeare* becomes particularly useful by including line references within the running heads.

The greatest diversity in layout among the editions in this survey, however, lies undoubtedly in their respective methods of presenting explanatory notes. *The New Penguin Shakespeare* is alone in separating notes entirely from the text itself and placing them at the back of the edition, and most students seem to regard this as a considerable disadvantage.

Of the editions which seek to make notes more immediately accessible, *The Arden Shakespeare, The New Cambridge Shakespeare* and *The Oxford Shakespeare* all adopt the essentially similar format of positioning notes in double columns at the foot of each page of text. Both *The Oxford Shakespeare* and *The New Cambridge Shakespeare* print the footnote word or phrase in bold, which makes for greater clarity and speed of identification than *The Arden Shakespeare* practice of italicising the word or phrase in question. The print in *The Oxford Shakespeare* footnotes however – although clear and well-spaced – is extremely small.

The remaining four editions offer facing-page notes. *The Macmillan Shakespeare* prints the footnoted word in roman and the notes themselves in italics. *The Kennet Shakespeare, The New Swan Shakespeare* and *The New Swan Shakespeare, Advanced Series* do the reverse. The most significant variation between these editions, however, is in the actual positioning of the notes. *The New Swan Shakespeare*, in what appears to be a rather perverse use of space, presents its notes in double columns of tiny print. Moreover, this edition also uses a system of reference that seems to me highly undesirable: annotations are signalled, not by line references as is normal practice, but by an entirely separate series of numbers which are scattered within the main text itself to produce a very unsatisfactory patchwork of words and figures. *The New Swan Shakespeare, Advanced Series* also disrupts the text in a way that does not appear especially constructive. In this case, a series of asterisks is used within the text, and the notes themselves carry line references. However, since these notes are printed as a block, rather than directly opposite the relevant passages, locating an individual reference becomes a much more elaborate procedure than ought to be necessary.

The Macmillan Shakespeare edition of *Othello* also offers its facing-page notes as a block, rather than in direct conjunction with the text, but the standard policy of the series as a whole appears to be to position notes as close as possible to the actual line under discussion. This is unfailingly the case with the notes in *The Kennet Shakespeare*, and the resultant clarity is without doubt a major strength of the series. *The Kennet Shakespeare* also introduces an effective variation on conventional practice by placing the music to songs directly opposite the lyrics themselves. (The *Macmillan* editions of *Twelfth Night* and *A Midsummer Night's Dream* are both – disappointingly – without music altogether.)

ILLUSTRATIONS constitute the third main area of presentation that will often influence the prospective buyer in selecting a particular edition, both on general aesthetic grounds of visual attractiveness and also on grounds of practical usefulness. This said, however, it must be conceded that inept or poor quality illustrations can deter at least as powerfully as appealing illustrations can entice. So perhaps it is for this reason that *The Macmillan Shakespeare*, *The New Arden Shakespeare* and *The New Penguin Shakespeare* have chosen to offer no illustrative material at all – an editorial policy, I am inclined to think, that *The Kennet Shake-*

speare and *The New Swan Shakespeare* might also be well advised to follow.

Of these two series, *The Kennet Shakespeare* is certainly the better-intentioned: its graphics are not confined solely to plot illustration (although Macbeth's bloody head puts in an inevitable appearance) but do attempt also to clarify certain aspects of production practice. But the quality, both of the artwork itself and of its reproduction, is undeniably poor. The final plate in the edition of *Romeo and Juliet* is so dark as to be indecipherable, and the illustration accompanying Act Five, Scene One of *As You Like It* transforms Arden into something out of 'The Beano'. *The New Swan Shakespeare*, on the other hand, although admittedly an edition designed especially for students of English as a second language, seems to see no function for pictures other than to transform the text into a kind of illustrated dictionary. In *Julius Caesar*, for example, 'Give me a bowl of wine' is obediently accompanied by a drawing of a drinking cup; owls, oaks, awls, doublets and a disconcertingly cheerful–looking bear are all laboriously depicted, and we are presented with a solemn visual lecture on the differences between a crown and a coronet.

After all this, *The New Swan Shakespeare, Advanced Series, The Oxford Shakespeare* and *The New Cambridge Shakespeare* – all of which (with the mysterious exception of the *Oxford* edition of *The Taming of the Shrew*) make intelligent use of maps, photographs and staging diagrams – come as a profound relief. *The New Cambridge Shakespeare* is particularly outstanding in this respect. The edition of *Othello*, for example, amid a wealth of fascinating material, provides contemporary maps of Venice and of Cyprus; detailed sketches showing possible methods of staging Act One, Scene Three and both scenes of Act Five; and a wonderfully well–chosen picture gallery presenting the most famous Iagos, Desdemonas and Othellos (both 'Arab' and 'Negro') of stage history.

Content

The obvious point at which to begin here, of course, is with the TEXT itself. And a very clear distinction can swiftly be drawn between those editions which are directed primarily towards an academic market and those which are aimed at a more general readership and are consequently less concerned with the minutiae of textual scholarship. *The New Swan Shakespeare*, *The Kennet Shakespeare* and *The Macmillan Shakespeare* all fall (to slightly different degrees) within the latter category: they present their texts free of variant readings (although *The Kennet Shakespeare* and *The Macmillan Shakespeare* may make occasional references to these within individual explanatory notes) and offer no substantial explanation of how each version has evolved. *The Kennet Shakespeare* editors all admit frankly that their texts amount simply to amalgams of existing editions; *The Macmillan Shakespeare* contents itself with a very short preface or 'Note on the Text'; *The New Swan Shakespeare* edition of *Julius Caesar*, taking textual reticence to something of an extreme, opts not even to mention the text at all.

The New Penguin Shakespeare, offering with each play an extremely lucid 'Account of the Text' and an appendix of collations, forms an interesting bridge between these three series and the remaining four series in this sample, which have all been prepared very specifically with advanced readers in mind. Indeed, the *New Penguin* seems to me considerably superior in this respect to *The New Swan Shakespeare, Advanced Series*, which rather high-handedly decides not to muddle its readers with too much information ('. . . much space in other editions is sometimes given to alternative readings of the text and to various conjectural explanations of difficult passages. Almost all speculation of this kind is omitted here.' – Bernard Lott, General Editor). Fortunately, however, *The Arden Shakespeare*, *The New Cambridge Shakespeare* and *The Oxford Shakespeare*, have no such scruples about protecting us from uncertainties.

All three of these series devote extensive and painstaking editorial space to examining in detail the difficulties – indeed, the impossibilities – of achieving a wholly 'reliable' text, and to analysing closely the differences between Folio and Quarto readings for individual plays (*The New Cambridge Shakespeare* does so in a 'Textual Analysis' section at the end of the edition; the others incorporate the material within the main Introduction itself); all three list variant readings at the foot of each page of text, and add appendices where appropriate (both the *Oxford* and the *New Cambridge* editions of *The Taming of the Shrew*, for example, append the additional Christopher Sly 'scenes' absent from the First Folio); and – most importantly – all three (especially the newer *Oxford* and *New Cambridge* series) reveal an increasing acceptance of the view that Shakespeare's own constant revision of his plays should be seen as a valid editorial yardstick. *The New Cambridge Shakespeare* edition of *Othello* rejects totally the notion of the existence of a so-called 'definitive text' and moves frequently between F and Q readings ('which the present editor believes represent two Shakespearean versions of the play'). More radically still, *The Oxford Shakespeare* edition of *Henry V* presents a controversial critical reevaluation – both of the text itself and of assumptions about textual authority – by following the supposedly 'Bad' Quarto in the Agincourt scenes. Moreover, this is shortly to be followed, so I'm told, by a *Hamlet* that will be strikingly and fundamentally different from any text to have preceded it. Heady days, indeed.

Just as the degree of textual explication varies from series to series to meet the needs and expectations of its prospective readership, so, too, do both the quantity and the nature of the EXPLANATORY NOTES that accompany the texts. So, again, it is probably fairest to assess the strengths of particular series in relation to others which seem to have been designed to cater for essentially similar requirements.

The New Swan Shakespeare is in one sense in a class of its own here, since not only is it intended primarily for non-native English speakers but it also aims to provide all textual explanation within a controlled vocabulary of 3000 words. The notes accompanying the text in *New Swan* editions take the form of scene summaries and of vocabulary glosses (inexplicably printed within inverted commas, as though actual quotations). In addition, a separate glossary is also given at the end of the text itself, in order to explain words 'which are used in Modern English as they were in Shakespeare's day, but are not among the 3000 most-used words in the language'. Inevitably, this restrictive formula can – and sometimes does – result in gross over-simplification. In general, however, the volume editors appear to have approached the task with a refreshing lack of cynicism and a genuine will to elucidate, for most of the notes are presented with admirable clarity.

Appropriately, given that they are obviously intended for a more sophisticated readership than *The New Swan Shakespeare*, *The Kennet Shakespeare*, *The Macmillan Shakespeare* and *The New Penguin Shakespeare* do not provide scene summaries within their support material, although both *The Kennet Shakespeare* and *The Macmillan Shakespeare* provide brief but helpful indications of how each particular scene might be staged, and all three series are very reliable in commenting – where appropriate – on the technical structure of an individual scene or on the way in which particular episodes of the plot relate to the play as a whole. Textual notes themselves – although inevitably there are fluctuations in standards among the different editors (the notes to the *Macmillan* edition of *Twelfth Night*, for instance, seem to me rather out of line with the series as a whole and, at points, inappropriate for school use) – are of a very high quality in all three series. My own preference is for the notes supplied in *The Kennet Shakespeare*, which interweave commentary on character, theme and imagery very skilfully with linguistic exegesis, but I am also impressed by the integration of useful source and background information within the *New Penguin* notes.

Of the four editions which cater for a more advanced market, *The New Swan Shakespeare, Advanced Series* – although lacking the scholarly edge of its competitors – undoubtedly provides the textual notes that are of greatest practical value to an average Sixth Form student. They make no unrealistic assumptions about prior knowledge, and concentrate simply on offering a clear, consistent and very closely detailed explanation of each play's language. *The Arden Shakespeare, The Oxford Shakespeare* and *The New Cambridge Shakespeare,* as one might expect, provide textual notes that are discerning, illuminating and academically impressive. But a reader in active need of support material in order to understand the text itself could sometimes be forgiven for finding them intimidating (*The Arden Shakespeare* takes 1200 words to explain ten lines of *Macbeth*) or pompous ('Aphorisms about opportunities irretrievably lost abound from antiquity' is *The Oxford Shakespeare*'s gloss for 'There is a tide in the affairs of men').

As a final point, I shall now turn briefly to the INTRODUCTIONS within each series – by which I mean all other editorial material supplementary to the footnotes, textual information and illustrations already considered, irrespective of whether it is placed before or after the text itself. Here, direct comparison focusing on different editions of the same individual plays seems to be the most appropriate method, so I shall conclude by examining four separate editions of *Julius Caesar* (as a representative O-Level play) and four separate editions of *Othello* (as a representative A-Level play).

The introductions to both the *Kennet* and the *New Swan* editions of *Julius Caesar* are very short. In the case of *The Kennet Shakespeare,* however, this is because of the series policy of including editorial commentary within the facing-page notes rather than through any dearth of ideas: on the contrary, the material offered in conjunction with the text is lively, interesting and discriminating. By contrast, the *New Swan* introduction (which includes a plot synopsis, brief notes on structure, staging and characters, and some very heavy-footed explanation of blank verse and imagery) must inevitably seem rather limited and old-fashioned.

The Oxford Shakespeare and *The Arden Shakespeare* editions of *Julius Caesar* both offer very extensive and informative introductions, giving considerable weight, for instance, to Shakespeare's use of source material and appending the relevant passages from North's *Plutarch*. The fundamental differences between their respective approaches, however, provide a fascinating demonstration of the shifting trends of critical thought that have characterised the last thirty years. The more conventional *Arden* introduction (first published in 1955) concentrates its intellectual energies very firmly on intimate psychologically-rooted character analysis, and above all on interaction with the *written* word. *The Oxford Shakespeare*, on the other hand, reflecting the preoccupations that have dominated the last decade, not only focuses sharply on the political, rather than the individual, but also places its emphasis very firmly on the play *in performance*. 24 pages are devoted to stage history, and an absorbing appendix deals in close detail with the difficulties surrounding one individual stage direction.

Both the *Macmillan* and the *New Penguin* editions of *Othello* offer excellent value for money [*Penguin* £1.10; *Macmillan* (now also retailing in bookshops) £1.50]. Each of them offers a highly informative, stylish and lucidly structured introduction, setting students a fine example in the management of illustrative textual detail, and both also append the music for the songs. *The New Penguin Shakespeare* introduction is presented as a continuous essay (although I wonder whether A-Level students might welcome sub-headings, or at least an index and appropriate running heads?), and the introduction is then supplemented by an extremely helpful Further Reading section. *The Macmillan Shakespeare* introduction, which is prefaced by an index, is perhaps more immediately accessible to students seeking quick reference because of its use of sub-headings: its Further Reading section, however, lacks the detail and direct guidance which make the *New Penguin* reading list so useful. The content of both introductions is essentially similar: both include commentary on the play's source, on the double time scheme, and on the characterisation of Othello and Iago. In addition, *The New Penguin Shakespeare* edition incorporates a wide frame of reference to critical opinion and to Shakespeare's other plays, and presents an ordered analysis of *Othello*'s imagery; *The Macmillan Shakespeare* edition offers a discussion of the racial issue, and also provides supplementary information on Venice.

The New Swan Shakespeare, Advanced Series is in many ways similar to the previous two series, although directed more specifically and exclusively at an A-Level readership. The introduction is divided into two sections. The first part consists of a general introductory essay on *Othello* (using sub-headings), which deals clearly and unpretentiously with the standard material on political and social background, source, and time-scale, and also supplies a very useful guide to the Elizabethan theatre. The second part contains a series of articles which are intended to encourage students to broaden their knowledge and which include discussions of principal characters, extracts of literary criticism and accounts of *Othello* in performance. An emphasis on these two latter concerns – in the form of detailed descriptions of *Othello*'s critical and stage histories – is the main hallmark which distinguishes *The New Cambridge Shakespeare* edition so very notably from the other three editions under consideration here, which, given their role as school texts, can inevitably devote only very limited space to topics that as yet seem to arouse very little interest in examination setters. It is an outstanding edition – scholarly, incisive and informative. I fully recommend it.

Conclusions

So which Shakespeare should one choose? Firstly, of course, it will depend to a great extent on the *level* at which the text is to be studied by the teaching group. One of the more scholarly editions would clearly be inappropriate and probably also rather intimidating for use with most school or college pupils below the age or ability of Advanced Level students. A second consideration, if one is thinking in terms of class use, must inevitably be the relative *cost* of the different editions. With these two factors in mind, my own inclinations would be as follows:

For non-examination students of Shakespeare

For general readers of Shakespeare, seeking an uncluttered text with helpful editorial material, nevertheless, available as required, *The New Penguin Shakespeare* is ideal – both for older students reading additional plays as a back-up to their main examination text and also for younger readers who might find facing-page notes a needless distraction.

For CSE, Ordinary or GCSE Level students

For students of English as a second language, the most appropriate edition is clearly *The New Swan Shakespeare*. For general use, however, largely on the grounds of layout, I would opt for either *The Kennet Shakespeare* or *The Macmillan Shakespeare* – with a slight preference for the editorial commentary of the former and the presentation of the latter.

For Advanced Level students

For students of very high academic ability for whom price was not a significant factor, the most useful and appropriate edition would obviously be either *The Arden Shakespeare*, *The New Cambridge Shakespeare* or *The Oxford Shakespeare*. Personally, I have a slight preference for the latter two series, but my final decision would undoubtedly be guided by making direct comparisons between the three editions in question, and selecting the edition whose introductory material seemed to me most interesting and stimulating. For average or low ability students, again if cost were irrelevant, my first choice would be *The New Swan Shakespeare, Advanced Series*. But for general, low-budget Sixth-Form use, *The Macmillan Shakespeare* – with its facing-page notes, high-quality introductory material and attractive presentation – seems to me to offer unbeatable value.

What's the Good?
Personal reflections on Shakespeare as a travelling companion

BOB FOWLER

' "What is the use or function of poetry nowadays?" is a question not the less poignant for being defiantly asked by so many stupid people or apologetically answered by so many silly people.' (Robert Graves in his foreword to *The White Goddess*, Faber)

This year, and increasingly every year, tens of thousands of young people in England alone will live with copies of Shakespeare plays as part of their daily lives. The Shakespeare industry will thrive, as Stratford England and Stratford Ontario flourish. Shakespeare summer schools will be over-subscribed. Private houses and gardens will stage Shakespeare plays. TV will include Shakespeare and introductions to Shakespeare in its winter season. Live and canned performances will be available in a wide range of styles, from Russian films of *Hamlet* to Toyah Wilcox in *The Tempest*. Hundreds of thousands of Shakespeare Study Aids will be sold, including photographic histories of previous productions, with glowing details of stage designs, sets and costumes, with intimate details revealed by researchers, such as plans to light Titania's brassière by means of a power supply concealed in her briefs. A rich business, and of undoubted good, at least to the economy.

Nevertheless, the majority of people in the world have had no acquaintance with Shakespeare. Would the world

be a better place if everyone carried a couple of Shakespeare plays in their baggage? Would it be worse if no
one knew Shakespeare? Even if the world were no worse
off, would I be? The late Roy Plomley allowed all his
castaways to have the complete works of Shakespeare in
addition to the Bible on their desert island. What's the
use?

'Use', in a literary context, has carried particular
connotations ever since Richard Hoggart gave the title
The Uses of Literacy to his seminal work. 'Good' has
rather a longer history. There are those who will
conclude that there is no *sensible* way to talk about good
except through allegory. Then, the *Pilgrim's Progress*
model becomes the vehicle for useful and moral Art.

There has been implicit in our culture and traditions
and institutions the idea that knowledge of the Arts of
civilisation is a good thing. The better the act (or higher,
though the cosmological residence of the good has been
less directional since Bishop Robinson's *Honest to God*),
the better the thing. To know the works of Shakespeare,
to know the works of Bach, to know the works of Michelangelo has been, to some, the indication not only of 'a
good education' but also of 'a good man'. Decline the
quality and doubts begin. Wagner is problematical,
Céline, later, more so. What happens to Ian Fleming?
Tom Sharpe? The Sex Pistols? Better stick to
Shakespeare.

Objective arguments to support the thesis that Shakespeare is useful in the good education sense are, however,
hard to find. Educationists tend to talk in terms of
'humanising and civilising influences' and 'modifying the
grain of our being'. On the other hand, others, like
George Steiner, have been remorseless in pushing the
question (regarded as quite irrelevant by some) 'Why did
the Arts fail us before the night?' (generally interpreted
to mean, 'Why do men who know good art allow bad
things – like the holocaust?'). At the same time another
aspect of the debate has become focused 'To do good work
has the artist got to be a good man as well as a good
artist?' An additional question might be 'Does making
good art make the artist good?' If not, what would be the

arguments for defending the case that to know good art is a good thing?

What does a man who knows Shakespeare have that a man who is ignorant of Shakespeare does not have? If it is impossible to answer that question *sensibly*, but one takes as a working hypothesis that it might be 'better' (more useful) to travel with Shakespeare (Bach, Michelangelo) than without him, what kind of knowledge of the works will best assist a pilgrim's progress? At what age might the companionship start?

My own earliest memory of acquaintance with Shakespeare came at about the age of 4, when an 11–year–old relation was preparing to play Cobweb in a first form annual Shakespeare production at a small Merseyside grammar school. I cannot remember whether or not I saw that production, but I remember vividly the homemade, simple, grey tabard with a black spider's web embroidered on it by Cobweb's mother. I think I might remember that it came to smell of greasepaint and excitement.

My next clear Shakespeare memory was at the age of 10, when our own year was performing *A Midsummer Night's Dream* at the same small school. I cannot remember whether or not I had a part, but certainly I was involved. It is one of the most vivid and important memories to me of my school, all Proust-madeleine. The Birkenhead Puck's lines I still hear to-day:

> Now the hungry lion roars,
> And the wolf behowls the moon;
> Whilst the heavy ploughman snores,
> All with weary task fordone.
>
> I am sent, with broom, before,
> To sweep the dust behind the door.

I do not know whether or not Puck spoke the lines with a Birkenhead accent.

Macbeth came our way by the third form in early preparation for School Certificate English Literature where it was the set text. I remember many hysterical sessions playing the three witches between the front desks and the master's dais. These are not important memories, insofar as they contributed little to my sensibility or appreciation of Shakespeare. It was only fifteen years later, when I directed a workshop on *Macbeth* with Nigerian teachers in Ibadan, that I came fully to understand the power of those weird sisters and their hold on Macbeth. Ten years later, Polanski again re-invested the sorcery within a credible, wild, unsophisticated context, to which I could respond.

At school, more vivid than playing witches and flinging imaginary eyes of newts and toes of frogs into non-existent cauldrons, were the single great events where whole forms, if not the whole school, were involved in visits to performances. The live performances were always over the water at the Liverpool Philharmonic, where great conductors talked, charmed or terrified us into listening and not coughing. I cannot remember the school ever going to see a live play, but the whole school (or so it seemed) went in 1944 to see Olivier's film of *Henry V* at the Birkenhead Gaumont. I was enthralled by so many aspects of the film that it would be difficult to list them all here. One memory, however, was especially significant: the audience infected each other with their response to the Henry/Katharine wooing scene. Whether we recognised nuances intuitively or whether we picked up the knowingness of the older pupils (I was a young twelve at the time) I do not know. What I remember is that as a result of our participation, our laughter, perhaps — who knows? — our wolf-whistles at the images on the screen, our behaviour was the subject of a whole school assembly the following morning. Of course, we blamed the boys from the neighbouring school. Nobody mentioned the girls from the Secondary Grammar School on the far side of the Park. What we learnt, in those closing stages of World War II, was not that Falstaff, babbling of green fields, might reflect the tears in mortal things, or even that Shakespeare might be used to re-kindle or inspire patriotic fervour, but that Shakespeare, even Shakespeare on film, could get you into trouble.

I leap now, like Shakespeare's chorus, over the years when I learnt to be bored by *Much Ado*; to understand the complicated pattern of curses working themselves in resolution in *Richard III*; to know that Shakespeare and Prospero had problems; to understand from Lear that the basest beggar is in the poorest thing superfluous; and to conclude that *Lear* is the greatest work of literature, though the Fool could often be tedious in performance. This leap covers some forty years to the present time when it is perhaps less easy, intellectually, to say the Anglican creed than ever before. Statements of belief are no less susceptible to challenge than they were in Galileo's day, although the Inquisition might show a different face, or employ different instruments of torture. Implicit beliefs are still held and defended without over–much objectivity. Meanwhile, the number of pupils taking examination courses in Drama and Theatre Arts has grown from nil to approaching forty thousand over the last ten years (in addition to the tens of thousands already following literature courses with Shakespeare set texts).

My outstanding memories of these latter years have been of discovering for the first time, in a performance by Sinead Cusack and Derek Jacobi, the wit of Beatrice and Benedick; of not being bored by Polonius when played by Tony Church; of being riveted by every line and gesture of Antony Sher's Fool until his death in a dustbin (so *that* was the answer to the question, 'What happened to Lear's fool?'!); of feeling the jingoism at a Gala performance of *Henry IV* during the Falklands war; of delighting in Joseph Marcell's black Puck, and crying again with laughter at Geoffrey Hutching's Bottom; observing adolescents, hardened to video horror, cowering at Bill Alexander's *Richard III*, while confessing to enjoying it more than Vincent Price, Theatre of Blood, and the variations of the Frankenstein, Dracula or Chainsaw presentations; of enjoying the visual delights of Ron Eyre's *Winter's Tale*; and, most recently, falling in love again with Katharine (Cecile Paoli) being wooed by King Harry.

The use, the good, the context of Shakespeare: do we

have to fall back on a creed as difficult to sustain in a common language as the virgin birth? Can we proceed in any way other than by assertion? In looking back over fifty years it seems that the old ways cannot serve, the old arguments cannot stand. The Arts and Shakespeare have their good and their uses; like knives and forks they are aspects of civilisation. Certainly we can do without them, but at the lowest *Recherche* denominator, I would not have missed the smell of greasepaint, even on Cobweb's costume. I would not have missed the trips in grottoes of words and lights and colours, and meetings with players in unknown lands and landscapes, the families and feuds, the romances and love-notes pinned on trees. I do not say, like the child who wrote to Thomas Mann, 'Your novel has helped me to live'. What I say, rather, is that Shakespeare has been a part and companion of my life and the questions we have exchanged on the way are closely to do with the uses and context and good of life. Value is implicit throughout the debate. There was a time when a man first climbed a mountain simply for pleasure. On the summit he might just admire the view, or he might find the tablets of the law or the lost Ark of the Covenant. The good, the use and context of Shakespeare is not unlike the good and use and context of mountains, which can be used for commando training, which can serve as uncrossable frontiers or barriers, but which cannot be ignored. In the twentieth century in England we have left our villages and isolation and become world travellers. But not just in England and the West are we travellers. We are all, whether we like it or not, on Pilgrim's journey. Shakespeare is part of the landscape, the theatre is a mode of transport, offering maps of terrain and travails to be crossed.

Shakespeare does not make people good. But he shows them what goodness is. He does not solve our problems, but he shows us what the problems might be. He does not make the choices for us, but he shows us what the choices are. If all meaningful thought is for action, then Shakespeare can aid thought and action. It is not a case of being silent about that which we cannot speak. Sophistication of thought can sometimes be Pilgrim's enemy in thought and action. Thus I give the last word to a contemporary ten–year–old, Robert. He is retelling the beginning of *Hamlet*, which he has translated into his own context, his own idiom of understanding. In addition to effective and poetic communication skills, one or two drafting slips apart, he shows he understands something about human problems, about relations, about Hamlet and about himself. The good of Shakespeare is revealed, I believe, in Robert's response to Hamlet. *Pace* Robert Graves, it stands without need of apology:

In 1600–1601 Hamlet – Prince of Denmark got a horrible [   ] his father died leaving a mystery because he was young kind and healthy and died so soon. Even more mysterious is that Gertrude his nice kind loving mother got married to Claudius his uncle soon after Hamlets father died. One night when Horatio = Hamlets best friend and two guards saw a ghost they challenged it, but it said nothing moments later it went into some rocks below the castle. The guards and Horatio were frightened it appeared again. Out of the ground it slowly came Horatio gathered his strength and went towards it "I challenge you, speak coward" it got closer Horatio recognised the armour and moustach. his mouth opened and he disapeared
"thats Hamlets fathers ghost" said Horatio
"Dont be stupid" said one of the guards "it is" "hes got the same armour, the same moustach"
"I think he'll only talk to hamlet" said Horatio
"well lets tell him and get it over with" said the over guard so all three went to get Hamlet.
Horatio knocked on Hamlets door "come in" he said
"Oh Hamlet your Majesty" said a guard "Horatio wants to tell you something"
"send him in" said Hamlet
"Hamlet we just saw your fathers ghost" said Horatio
"What did he say?" said Hamlet
"nothing, I think he'll only talk to you" said Horatio

"Where is he now?" said Hamlet

"We saw him while on guard" said Horatio "we challenged him but he said nothing" said a guard.

"I'll come on guard with you tomorrow night" said Hamlet. so the next night Hamlet ate his Roast Swan and sylabob "see you tommorow mum" said Hamlet

"what about the vegetables" she said.

"I'm not that hungry" he said

You'll eat your vegetables like it or not" said Claudius.

So he ate the vegetables and went.

"Your late" said Horatio

"Claudius made me eat everything on my plate" said Hamlet

"He appeared two minutes ago" said a guard

"where is he" said Hamlet

"over there" said the other guard

"Father, your Majesty" said Hamlet.

The Ghost said nothing "look hes pointing over there"

"Follow me son" said the ghost

"dont go hamlet" said Horatio

"I have to" said Hamlet

"he probably wants you fall over the castle walls and perish on the rocks" said a guard

Hamlet ripped free "I have to follow him" said Hamlet. Hamlets father led Hamlet to a dark corner in the watch tower.

"I want you to kill claudius son" "But why" said Hamlet

"he killed me and has taken my wife".

"How did claudius kill you dad" Asked Hamlet

"One Autumn day I had just written a letter to the King of England i Lay down on my couch". "Claudius came up to me while I was asleep and poured poison down my ear"

"How did you know it was Claudius" Asked Hamlet

"The poison was cold as soon as it touched my ear i woke up he ran away the poison went to my brain and all down my vains all over my body causing intense pain". "The Doctors could'nt cure me and i died".

"What do you want me to do?" said Hamlet.

"I didn't have time to pray God to get rid of my sins so I went to hell"

"what is hell?" asked Hamlet

"it is a fiery place of evil where they take away your sins" said the Ghost "kill Claudius for this, please will you promise me".

Hamlet couldnt say no. The Ghost dissapeared Hamlet sighed and went to his room.

Hamlet now has a problem he has promised to kill Claudius but he knows it is wrong and has to think of away to hide his anger from Claudius. So, he pretends to be mad so he can kill Claudius with out being suspected. Hamlet has another problem now he has fallen in love with Ophelia the daughter of polonius, the kings advisor. So Polonius reminded Ophelia that Hamlet was a prince and will marry a princess not a girl like her. Hamlet sat down on his bed and thought about his problems – especially his new problem. Hamlets last problem of the day was wondering whether the ghost was his father or an evil spirit from Hell.

[This personal reflection is not a statement of HMI view, advice or judgment.]